SPIRITL

MW01493729

"This is the only book I have ever seen that seamlessly combines spiritual laws and sales. This is not about techniques; it shows you how to make internal changes that will impact your outside world. For my money, this is the best book out there for entrepreneurs and salespeople."

—Dr. Joe Vitale, author of *The Attractor Factor* and *Zero Limits*

"In this book, Spiritual Selling, Joe Nunziata has discovered the secrets to success and abundance: that they come from within and are created by your thoughts and feelings. His techniques are easy to follow and essential in helping you attain your true business potential. He knows that being successful is not about how many hours you work, but rather about how you see yourself on your most basic level."

—Susan Kerr, spiritual counselor and author of *The System for Soul Memory*

"If you are tired of the push and pull that come with traditional methods of selling, Joe Nunziata's book Spiritual Selling is a must have. The principles Joe teaches are based on attraction rather than force. His approach is not some pie-in-the-sky theory. Rather, he skillfully shows how you can begin attracting business to you rather than chasing after it—more business than you dreamed possible. Regardless of what you sell, this book will enlighten you in ways you never imagined."

—Kathleen Gage, author of *The Law of Achievement*

"Spiritual Selling is an essential book for every person in sales. It delivers a message that everyone should hear. It is clear, concise and makes it easy to put the principles to work. Joe Nunziata is a genius at teaching others how to reach the next level. I recommend that this be required reading by everybody in sales."

—Rhonda L. Sher, author of The 2 Minute Networker

"It is not difficult to be a good salesperson, but to be great you need an edge. Joe Nunziata's Spiritual Selling is that edge. The strategies Joe outlines make perfect sense and are easy to implement. Joe shows you how to work from the inside out so you can stop chasing money. All you need is the desire to be great and the persistence to follow the step-by-step plan. Getting to great has never been easier."

—Richard Parker, president of Diomo Corporation; author of the best-selling How to Buy a Good Business at a Great Price and faculty member of Trump University

"The days of the hard sell are over. In order to succeed today and to enjoy your career in sales, you need to position yourself to get people to come to you. That is exactly what Joe teaches you how to do in Spiritual Selling. Hey, it worked for me!"

—Robert Levin, Editor-in-Chief and Publisher, The New York Enterprise Report

"Spiritual Selling takes an entirely new approach to selling. Instead of chasing down the sale, the principles taught in this book will have people chasing you down to do business. And these same principles work to dramatically enhance your personal life as well. This book is a must read for the business professional."

—David Frey, CEO of Marketing Best Practices Inc.; author of The Small Business Marketing Bible

"While there is no shortage of books and programs out there about how to sell, Joe Nunziata's, Spiritual Selling is the first one in ages to offer something truly new and different.   His "sales attractor " method will dash many common stereotypes about successful salespeople. Highly recommended for anyone looking for something new about selling in the 21st century."

Spiritual SELLING 2.0

Attract Your Ideal Clients NOW

JOE NUNZIATA

LBF
Publishing

Published LBF Publishing
Clearwater, FL

Paperback ISBN: 978-0-9701615-2-9
Ebook ISBN: 978-0-9701615-1-2

To Maria—thank you for your incredible support and unconditional love.

CONTENTS

FOREWORD

If you're trying to make sales and running into dead ends, the problem may not be with your product, your service, or your prospect. It may in fact have to do with an invisible block within you.

After all, there are countless books out there on how to be a better salesperson. If all the techniques worked, why aren't people making more sales?

Again, the answer is within.

It may be tough to accept at first, but a lack of results has more to do with your own inner nature than it does with outer circumstances. This book helps you uncover your inner blocks and gives you the tools to clear them.

As I wrote in my book *The Attractor Factor*, until you get clear of these internal blocks to success, you will have a tough go of it. You'll blame the world for your poor sales when the real responsibility is within yourself.

If that's so, what do you do about it? How do you get clear?

This book reveals Joe's secret to success. For my money, this is the best book out there for entrepreneurs and salespeople. It shows you where the snags are, and it reveals what to do about them. If you want to solve your sales problems and make the living you dream about, you've come to the right place.

Pull up a chair and listen as Joe Nunziata reveals the ultimate secrets to sales success.

—Dr. Joe Vitale

ABOUT THE AUTHOR

Joe Nunziata is an internationally known speaker and author. He has been delivering his life-changing message at events and seminars since 1992. Joe has been working in the areas of personal development and human potential for over thirty years. His unique blend of psychology, philosophy, spirituality, and the power of energy is designed to foster a new way of thinking in business and in life.

Joe has always recognized the importance of working from within. He teaches that to be truly successful, you must make powerful internal changes and break destructive patterns of behavior. These unconscious patterns are connected to deep emotional energy that must be changed to facilitate long-term success in all areas of life.

In 1992, Joe founded Joe Nunziata International as a personal development company. Today Joe offers consulting, training, public seminars, and products on business and personal development. Joe is available for both public and private engagements by appointment only.

Other books and programs include *Chasing Your Life, Finding Your Purpose, Karma Buster, No More 9 to 5*, and *Elevate Your Energy, Elevate Your Life*.

Joe has appeared on television programs including *Good Day New York* on Fox, Gaiam TV, Better TV, and *News 12 Long Island*, plus various radio stations including KFNN (Phoenix, AZ); KTHO (Sacramento, CA); KCEO (San Diego, CA); KLMO (Denver, CO);

WXCT (Hartford, CT); WPLC (Washington, D.C.); WOKB (Orlando, FL), and many others.

To find out more, visit Joe's web site at **www.JoeNunz.com** and **www.spiritualselling.com**.

YouTube Channels
SpiritualSelling.TV
aShotofJoe.com

INTRODUCTION

WELCOME TO Spiritual Selling 2.0!

Spiritual Selling 2.0 introduces new concepts and principles to the world of sales and business. It includes new content plus an updated version of my book *Spiritual Selling*, which was published in September 2007. Many people said the book was ahead of its time back then. Some people loved the concept, others were confused, some were a bit scared, and the old-school hardcore sales dudes dismissed the idea as weird, new-age nonsense.

I received a message from my original publisher giving the rights of the book back to me. This got me thinking; maybe it was time to release an updated version of this book for the new world of business.

The energy of the world has shifted dramatically since 2007. People are seeking more fulfilling ways to live and work. We are moving to a higher level of consciousness and the old rules of business and sales no longer apply. This is a process we have been experiencing for some time now. There is a lot of shifting and changing taking place in the world. This is happening to us as individuals and on a global scale.

Now is the time to embrace a new way to live and work as we move from a "me consciousness" to a "we consciousness." Some are ready to elevate while others will remain in their old energy and beliefs. There is no need for judgment. We all have free will here on Earth, and each person has the right to make their own choices. Follow your instinct and trust that the universe will guide you for your highest and greatest good.

The new *Spiritual Selling 2.0* content is followed by an updated version of the original *Spiritual Selling* book. The new section addresses the changes we are experiencing and will continue to feel as we move forward.

Enjoy your journey to higher energy and greater success!

This book will introduce you to new concepts and philosophies that will completely transform the way you view sales, business, and life. *Spiritual Selling* combines the power of spiritual principles and the laws of energy with proven sales and marketing strategies. This approach resulted in the development of the Attractor Sales System™. This unique process is designed to turn you into a magnet for new business and abundance.

The word *abundance* has been associated with the acquisition of money and material possessions in many books and publications. Attracting more wealth is a wonderful aspect of this process, but it is not the only thing you will receive. The principles in this book will also aid you in attracting more fulfilling relationships, improved health, and, most importantly, a state of peace and joy. As you integrate these principles into your business you will see a change in other areas of your life. The universal principles you will discover can be applied successfully to any area of your life.

I have spent over thirty years in sales and marketing. Most of my work has taken place on the mean streets of New York City. I have sold everything from women's shoes and satellite dishes to print advertising space and cable spots. After working in retail, service, and wholesale for large corporations and small businesses, I realized the sales game is pretty much the same. I wrote this book to help all my friends who are out there fighting the good fight every day.

When I first entered the world of sales, I was introduced to new definitions and concepts. The first terms I learned to describe salespeople were *hunters* and *farmers*. A hunter is a person who aggressively attacks the market in search of new business. The farmer is a relationship builder who uses a softer approach.

In my years of experience, I have encountered many different types of salespeople. Most have fallen into three main categories:

1. *Motivated by money.* There are certain individuals who do not care about what they sell. They are motivated by money and money alone. Although I have encountered some very successful people in this category, I do not suggest it as a course of action. These people were heartless mercenaries who would run you over in the parking lot to beat you to a potential sale. If this is the strategy to which you subscribe, this is not the book for you.

2. *Must love what you sell.* These people must have a deep emotional connection and love for what they sell. It is not about money, although these are the most successful of all salespeople, but more about how they can help make the world a better place. If you like this concept, this is the book for you.

3. *Why am I here?* Some folks don't seem to know how or why they landed in sales. It may have seemed like a good way to make money, or maybe they weren't qualified for anything else. In some cases, it was a last resort. If you are confused, this book will help you gain some clarity and possibly put you on the right path.

I have added a new category, "the attractor," to the list. Attractors focus their energy on drawing the right people to them. This book will show you how to stop chasing new business and start attracting it like never before.

Most organizations train salespeople to attack like predators. A lion is one of the most feared predators in the animal kingdom. Every day the lion goes out and stalks prey, hiding in the trees and bushes. Antelopes are the favorite prey for a lion. When a herd of unsuspecting antelopes strolls by, the lion waits for just the right moment. Then it jumps out and attacks. The lion chases antelopes until it catches and kills what is needed to eat for the day. The next day the lion gets up and starts the process all over again.

Sound familiar?

Many potential customers run from salespeople the same way antelopes run from lions. Do you feel like you are always chasing prospects, trying to get new business? Are you the predator chasing your prey just to stay alive . . . to hunt for another day? Do you feel exhausted by this process?

Now imagine you are trying to catch bees. You could buy a net and run around trying to catch one bee at a time. Or you could put some honey out to attract bees in large numbers. The honey would allow you to attract hundreds of bees at a time. Would you rather be the chaser (predator) or the attractor?

The honey, in this analogy, is your ability to vibrate the energy necessary to attract the perfect client. You will become the provider of choice in your category of business because of the feelings you are sending to the universe. As you will see, your success has a lot more to do with how you feel and a lot less to do with your actions.

When your true purpose is to help others, you change the way you are perceived and you elevate your energy vibration. Your customer can sense if you are focused exclusively on money and numbers. Focus on helping people and watch your magnetism expand.

I learned early in my sales career that I wanted to be the attractor. I saw too many salespeople burn out constantly chasing business. They looked as though they had been through a war, fighting to keep their numbers up. Many were tired, irritable, and in a state of constant distress.

Rightly, selling is the most fun you will ever have in the business world. There is nothing more exciting than closing your first big deal. The entire process should be fun and exhilarating, not a torturous grind that might eat you alive. Using the Attractor Sales

System™ will restore the fun and excitement to your business or career in sales. You will begin to think, feel, and act differently.

All I ask is that you remain open to these new ideas about selling.

WHAT IF EVERYTHING YOU LEARNED ABOUT SALES IS WRONG?

Looking at society, it becomes abundantly clear that something has gone wrong—very wrong.

» Why do bad things seem to happen to good people?
» Why do nice guys finish last?
» Why are some not-so-nice guys doing very well?

As of this writing an alarming 76% of all wealth in the U.S. is being controlled by only 10% of households, 50% of households own just 1% of all wealth. Personal debt is expanding faster than most people's waistlines and there is no end in sight. These circumstances are the result of manipulation and the desire to control the population.

In a fair world, everyone who deserved a break would surely get one. In our current world, the rich get richer, and the poor keep on paying taxes. Successful salespeople seem to receive all the best leads, the best deals, and the best accounts. And, of course, we all know they make the most money. Why is it so easy for them and so difficult for most people?

Believe it or not, there are clear answers to all of these questions, and I do my best to resolve them in this book. The answers I present may contradict many of the things you have learned and believe. All I ask is that you keep an open mind to the possibilities that I present in the pages that follow.

My goal is simply this: to change your belief system and open your mind to a world you may not know exists. To enter this world you must be willing to accept certain new truths that may seem a bit "out there." Your openness will allow you to see things that you could not see in your old belief system.

When I first learned the principles I am going to share with you, I was in shock. This new philosophy was actually much simpler than the one I had previously learned. When things seem to be too easy, we have a tendency to think, "This can't be true." We have been conditioned to believe that most accomplishments are achieved with pain and suffering.

I do not mean to suggest that great achievements are attained without effort and dedication. Many successful people apply an incredible amount of energy to their work. What makes them successful is that they are working with *flowing* energy, not *forced* energy. When you are working with flowing energy, you can work twice as hard and never feel fatigued. This is why successful people all seem so energetic.

Successful people are locked in and congruent with their purpose. They do not wake up in the morning dreading the day. These people are not pushing a boulder up a mountain, hoping they won't slip and be crushed. This group is cruising along, picking up momentum at every turn. Their boulder is rolling downhill.

These people are living in a different energy. They get it! Most of the population spend their lives grinding it out.

The bottom line is most people are just a few slight adjustments away from creating a better life. When I learned these new principles, I could not believe how close I was to this major breakthrough. You will discover how a little fine-tuning in your belief system and energy level will be the catalyst to creating incredible changes in your business and personal life.

WHY COMPANIES CHOOSE TO TRAIN PREDATORS

Most organizations are shortsighted and want sales *now*. They are oriented to predators who must continually make sales to survive. The attractor focuses more energy on the big picture and growing the business. Once the attractor's system is built, it drives new business day after day, year after year. The Attractor Sales System™ takes time to develop. It may not produce results right away. The big question is, are you willing to take two steps back to take ten steps ahead?

Unfortunately, many people are not willing to take a few steps back to reflect on the big picture. This resulted in a high-pressure sales environment that created stress and anxiety. Believe it or not, many people unconsciously enjoy feelings of tension. These feelings create an adrenaline rush that people feed on like drugs or alcohol. Many people constantly need this feeling and continue to re-create high drama.

When you choose to become an attractor, you are choosing peace. I call this the *flow state*. This is a feeling that everything is simply flowing as it should and all you have to do is ride the current. Imagine flowing with the current of a river, as opposed to trying to swim against it. Swimming against the current is extremely difficult and eventually impossible to maintain. Going with the current is easier and requires less effort.

Many of us have been trained and conditioned to go to work and grind it out. In no environment is this more evident than sales. Managers, following orders, send the troops out on a search and destroy mission. This "take no prisoners" attitude creates tension and a loss of focus. Instead of paying attention to the main objective, the best interest of the customer, sales become a simple numbers game of attrition.

In this book I hope to change the way people think about sales and salespeople. These highly skilled and dedicated people have been portrayed in a negative light for many years. When you mention the word *salesperson*, many people think of a used car salesman and immediately conjure up a negative image. It's time to take sales to a higher level of consciousness for both salespeople and their customers.

Enjoy making the transition from predator to attractor. Your life and perception of sales will never be the same.

PART ONE

YOUR ENERGY

1

HIGH ENERGY SELLING

In 2006 I had an idea. At the time, I was working as a sales and marketing consultant in New York. I started my official career in sales in 1985. I realized later that I had been in sales all my life . . . just like you. We are always selling in this life, and it starts at a young age. You may be working on your parents for a later curfew or trying to get a date with someone special. In the end it always comes back to selling.

After years of the push and pull of corporate selling, I was ready for a change. I had been studying and applying energy principles in my personal life for some time, and my life was moving in a positive direction. Then it hit me—if these are universal energy principles, why can't I apply them to sales and business?

The big difference was the philosophy I discovered studying energy work versus the conventional sales training I received in corporate America. In the world of higher energy, it is all about helping people elevate and doing things that benefit all parties. Conventional selling was focused on getting the deal at all costs regardless of collateral damage.

Early in my career, I was enamored with the success stories of people like Cornelius Vanderbilt, John D. Rockefeller, and Andrew Carnegie. These guys built incredible business empires, from scratch, with determination and grit. Naturally, it made sense to follow in the footsteps of those who had blazed the trail.

I often pondered, how did these men overcome the odds to create such powerful business empires? I went on a quest to find as much information as I could about these business titans. I was searching for their formula for success. My research started as a fairytale but ended as a nightmare. As I dug deeper, I learned the truth about these men and how they achieved their levels of influence. Much of their success was the product of cutthroat deals and the abuse of workers.

In each case, these men had built their fortunes on the backs of their employees using ruthless tactics. This of course raised another important question; were these tactics the only way to become successful in this world? As I looked around, it certainly seemed that way. The people I knew who focused on money and power above all else seemed to be the most successful. As you would imagine, this was a very disturbing revelation.

I thought to myself, were the words of Michael Douglas, aka Gordon Gekko in the film *Wall Street,* "Greed is Good," accurate? It has become abundantly clear that we are living in a very unbalanced society headed for destruction. This is counter to the teachings I have been studying and living, for many years

How do we overcome thousands of years of conditioning to create an enlightened business environment and new world economy? It all begins with you. As each person steps across the line into this new world, we become stronger. Those on this path require the courage and resolve to remain strong amid the resistance you are sure to face. Holding on to your power and beliefs is critical when it comes to making positive changes.

Sales has always been a survival of the fittest game with no place for the faint of heart. The trick was adding the energy element while still holding on to core sales and business practices. It was walking a parallel path of good energy, ethics, and skill. To many, this concept was counterintuitive based on the success stories we grew up with post the Industrial Revolution, especially in the Western world.

We are working on two levels. I call it E squared:

Energy & Expertise

Energy	Expertise
» How You Feel » What You Believe » The Energy You Projecting » Your Feeling of Worthiness » What You Are Attracting	» Sales Process » Product Knowledge » Presentation Skills » Communication and Listening Skills » Consistency

The objective is blending high energy with expertise. Your feelings and beliefs are as important, if not more important, than your level of expertise. Knowing how you feel before each call or presentation will help you gain a greater understanding of the results you are currently creating.

MOVING TO HIGHER ENERGY

I have seen many salespeople with very high levels of skill and expertise who struggled to maintain a steady flow of sales. This may seem confusing to those of you who are more logical. If I have the skills and expertise how is possible to struggle? This is where the concept of energy comes into the picture. How a person feels plays a major role in their level of success.

This question opens the door to the world of energy and emotion. Will I be more effective when I feel better? The obvious answer is yes. If you feel excited, believe in what you are selling, and like the company, the results will follow. This may seem simple but there are many variables that can knock you off track. I meet many people who are very excited about a new business, job, or idea. They believe in it, work hard, and still struggle. How is that possible? Below the surface we all hold powerful unconscious beliefs and emotions. These deep emotions are responsible for the results you are creating.

I have encountered many hard-working people who struggle their entire lives. These people are holding the energy of struggle and unworthiness. No matter how hard they work or how excited they seem on the outside, their struggle continues. This raises another important question.

Is your energy more important than your work ethic and skill level?

Once again, the simple answer is yes . . . but. Higher energy will always win in the end, but having a strong work ethic and high skill level will accelerate your process dramatically.

In today's world, sales managers and executives are quick to explain why sales are up or down. Most of these explanations are tied to things here in the physical world like the economy, price point, and competition. These factors may have some effect, but they pale in comparison to the impact of your energy and beliefs. Do you ever think about the energy of the company and employees? How does it feel to work there and sell the product or service they offer?

We all project energy based on our feelings and beliefs. Let me go into some more detail regarding this topic. Your energy is constantly attracting and repelling. You will notice this more as you elevate your awareness. I have experienced this with many of my clients, not to mention family and friends. When you are feeling deserving and confident, you will attract great clients. If you feel unworthy and desperate, you will attract negative clients. It is important to keep a close eye on what type of people you are bringing in.

One of my clients, Tony, owns an accounting firm. One day he was telling me how annoying his clients are and how they never pay on time. Tony was in full victim mode. I asked, "Why are you attracting this type of client?" He immediately became defensive and fired back, "It has nothing to do with me; these people are deadbeats." This is a typical reaction, as most people have been conditioned to act as victims and give away their power. In high energy we accept responsibility for our lives and what we are creating. Tony held on to his victim status, and I stopped working with him shortly after that conversation.

How you feel before going into an appointment will determine the outcome. When you are feeling pressure and fear, that energy is felt by the prospect. You are sending that energy to the prospect before you get there. This is what I mean by seeing things from a higher perspective. Fear-based emotions repel people because they carry a negative vibration of energy.

NO PRESSURE

Pressure, like all things here in the physical world, has positive and negative aspects. As a kid who grew up to be a big sports fan in New York, I had the opportunity to see pressure firsthand. New York fans and the media can be brutal on professional athletes. It always amazed me how certain players rose to the occasion while others wilted under the pressure. What made these players so good in critical moments with the game on the line? Did these guys like the feeling of pressure? The simple answer is yes!

We all experience our emotions differently based on many factors including our childhood experience. If you had a stressful and difficult childhood, you are more prepared to deal with adversity. Overcoming obstacles is part of your DNA. Others are just naturally comfortable in stressful situations.

In sports, sales, and business, we all experience pressure. The key is how we process it. People who struggle absorb the feeling, which creates anxiety and stress. When you take it on as a responsibility, it becomes heavy and weakens your energy. This creates a feeling of resistance because you do not want the pressure.

The key to success is accepting and embracing pressure. This removes the resistance and tension, allowing the energy to flow through you. In this state, the feeling of pressure is elevating your energy to a higher level. This is how great athletes thrive under pressure.

There are certain things salespeople and organizations do that create negative feelings of pressure and stress.

These are the **Four Negative Pressure Points:**

Fear of Loss: In this case you are more afraid to lose a deal than make one. This feeling of fear is felt by your prospect, which repels the client.

Attachment to the Outcome: When you are only focused on the outcome, you are preoccupied with closing the deal, not offering the best value and service.

Expectations: There is nothing wrong with setting goals, but when you attach an expectation, you create a desired outcome based on your perspective. This limits your opportunity for higher levels of success.

Judgment: Prejudging a prospect creates a narrow view of the client and potential for growth.

Before you speak to your next prospect, be aware of your feelings and see if you are holding any of these four. All of these create unnecessary feelings of pressure and stress. When you walk into your next appointment without any of these feelings, you remove all pressure and resistance.

Focus on how you can help the prospect, make a connection, and allow the appointment to flow organically. You will be amazed at how this clear feeling of energy creates much better results.

BE HUMAN, PLEASE

A while back, I was shopping for a new car. It was the first time, I was able to purchase a nicer car, and I wanted to make a good choice. The internet was still new back then, so you had to shop the old-fashioned way. Walk around and stop in different car dealerships. As a sales trainer, I was always interested in the approach of the salesperson. One day I had two very different experiences back-to-back.

I entered the first dealership and was immediately met by a buttoned-up guy in his early forties. He was wearing a dark brown three-piece suit and had some dazzling jewelry including a garish watch and cufflinks. He was the definition of a car salesman. He proceeded to show me a car and did not stop talking for fifteen minutes straight. I was impressed with his lung capacity but not his style.

He was a "robo-salesperson." His script was exact, he looked perfect, and he hit on every key point. His knowledge of the product was excellent, and he delivered the information flawlessly. The problem was I felt like I was taking to robot . . . not a person.

It took me a few minutes to shake of the barrage I had just experienced. Then I proceeded to walk across the street to another dealership. When I first walked in, I was greeted by a woman at the front desk. She directed me to the lounge for coffee and snacks. She told me someone would be out to help me in a minute. I poured myself a cup of coffee and walked into the showroom area.

Within a few minutes, a slightly overweight guy in his fifties, wearing a nice polo shirt, came up to me and introduced himself. The next thing he did was start asking questions, but not about the car. He asked me things like, are you from the area and where did you grow up.

I told him I was originally from Brooklyn, and he was too; I think everyone in New York was originally from Brooklyn. We chatted for a few minutes and then he invited me to have a seat in his office. This was the first time we started to talk about the car. He asked me a few questions including:

» What car are you driving now?
» How will you be using the car?
» Do you take clients out?

We walked out into the showroom, and he directed me to a few options that fit my needs. I asked a few questions and told him I wanted to come back with my wife to get her feedback. This is where I was sold. At no point did he try to hard close me on the spot. He respected my position, and I made an appointment to come back a few days later with my wife.

Most salespeople in that situation are going to try to hard close you on the spot. They have been trained, by fear-based management, that if the person leaves, your chance of making the sale is dramatically reduced. In the old world that may have been true, but this will not be the case moving forward. My wife and I went back for our scheduled appointment and purchased the car. We referred several people and then purchased another car from the same salesman a few years later.

This was not a sales experience, it was a human experience. Connecting with another person and creating a comfortable situation is the key to selling at a higher level. Being aware of the emotional connection and feeling is not what most of us learned in the corporate sales world. It was all techniques and hard closing.

Selling with higher energy requires trust. You believe in what you are doing and know it will pay off in the long term. Walking the high road is not always easy. I have seen so many situations where people choose money over ethics. Hold the line and know you are on the right path.

SELLING FEAR

One of the oldest techniques in the game is selling fear. When you can create a fear of loss, people feel compelled to buy what you are selling. This is accomplished by telling people that if they don't buy what you have right now, something bad will happen to them or they will lose out.

Another technique is using scarcity to compel someone to buy. We only have thirty of these left, so you had better act now or your life will be ruined. There are modifications that can be used in a softer way. Maybe you are offering a product with limited availability. There is nothing wrong with saying we have a limited supply, or the sale ends on a certain day. This is simply stating the information, not attempting to scare someone into buying.

Why can't you just be straight, share your ideas, and see if you are a good match? You can, but you need faith and belief to live in this space. We have been conditioned to sell using pressure and fear.

Now is the time to shift to love and joy.

HIGHER GROUND

I have always loved the song Higher Ground by Stevie Wonder. My favorite line is:

I'm so glad that I know more than I knew then
Gonna keep on tryin'
Till I reach my highest ground

Reaching your highest ground takes work. You are required to have discipline and courage to continue your journey forward. This is something to strive for in the new world we live in. As each person lights up, we raise the vibration of the planet and create new paradigms. Taking the high road will become the normal course of action in business and your personal life.

As you hold the higher ground, you will encourage others to move along the same path. This will create a chain reaction of positive energy. Doing business from your heart will become the new normal.

There is bound to be resistance as many will fear these concepts. Remember, fear-based people have a strong desire to hoard knowledge, power, and money. Their greatest fear is there is not enough to go around. This is a ridiculous idea not based on reality.

Does it make sense for one person to have over a billion dollars while others are starving? I have nothing against people becoming successful and rich. One of the keys to creating a better world is wealth distribution. The world has been out of balance for thousands of years. As we elevate, there will be a more even distribution of wealth and resources.

I call this concept *Greater Goodism*. I have created a site and a Facebook page to help this movement get rolling. You can see more at **GreaterGoodism.com**.

Greater Goodism is the practice of making decisions that are in the best interest of all parties, including yourself.

We do not want to create a world of self-sacrificing martyrs. You are here to give and receive. Here we go back to balance. Make decisions that work for all parties when possible. In some cases, there are sacrifices to be made based on conditions and the big picture.

This is the old story of the captain on a sinking ship. Is it for the greater good to sacrifice 100 people to save 1000? The obvious answer is yes, but it is not easy to make that type of decision. Some of your greater good decisions will be very easy, while others will prove to be more challenging.

There is no perfect system here on earth. The key is your intention. Sometimes things do not work out as planned. There are many reasons for these outcomes, and all are tied to your journey. You came to have a certain experience and others involved came to have their own. This is not good or bad, it is just what it was meant to be.

When you enter a situation with a negative intention, you want to hurt someone. The desire to hurt another person is tied to your negative ego and unresolved emotional issues within yourself. We have all had an experience like this at one time or another. In this case, you were overtaken by a powerful emotion you were unable to resolve at the time.

Always remember, your energy is always moving and must go somewhere. When you are unable to deal with the emotions within yourself, it is natural to look for another way to release this energy. This is where a negative intention will surface. Be aware of how you are feeling before you take the first step. This will help you gain a deeper understanding of what you are truly feeling.

The gentlemen I spoke of earlier, Cornelius Vanderbilt, John D. Rockefeller, and Andrew Carnegie, were all focused on winning at all costs. Their intention was to win, no matter what. We all want to win but at what cost? This is where the concept of the greater good comes into play. Is winning worth the damage caused? In the military they call it collateral damage. We bombed that bunker to kill a terrorist but killed 300 innocent people in the process. Was it worth it?

People with negative or ego-based intentions will always find a way to justify their behavior. Using terms like, *there was no other way to do it,* is a common response. Another important thing to understand is people in this state do not feel remorse. They are only focused on the win. Anything in the way must be removed regardless of cost or casualties. It may be hard for you to comprehend how someone could operate this way. No judgment, please, we all see things from our own perspective. This is a world of positive and negative energy. We need both for the full experience.

The next time you are going to make a deal or partner with someone, be sure to check your intention and alignment. This will help you elevate to a higher level and create a positive outcome for all.

2

UPGRADING YOUR EMOTIONAL OPERATING SYSTEM

I know you are very concerned about making sure the operating systems of your devices are all up to date. You do this because you know they will run smoothly with the latest updates. Are you doing the same for your Emotional Operating System?

Everything you are creating in life is based on your emotions and beliefs. The ability to process your emotions properly will be a great asset to your career and life. Every sales call is an emotional encounter. The more you understand yourself emotionally, the faster you will go.

Your life reflects your emotional state of being. You have developed a system to deal with, and process, emotions based on what you learned as a child. Your specific Emotional Operating System is the result of many factors, including:

» Your DNA
» Your Karma

» Your parents
» How you learned to manipulate others
» How you learned to get what you want
» How you learned to survive
» What you learned from watching your parents

Most of us did not grow up in an environment where expressing emotions was safe or acceptable. In many cases, the display of emotion was met with criticism and ridicule. Human beings are designed to adapt and survive. Once you realize expressing your feelings is not safe, you naturally shut down your emotions as a defense mechanism. This protects you from negative energy and pain.

The result of this tactic is blocking your emotions. The only question is how you learned to avoid your feelings. The most common techniques are repression, self-criticism, compulsive behavior, becoming a victim, or acting out. Let's look at each of these and how they impact your life.

REPRESSION:

In this case, you have learned to push the emotions down. The problem is, your energy is always moving, and it must go somewhere. This blocked energy can manifest as illness, create accidents or other problems in your life. It can also move you into a state of depression.

SELF-CRITICISM:

You may have been trained to beat yourself up when things do not go as you hoped or expected. This creates internal stress and lowers your energy. You will also feel unworthy and undeserving.

COMPULSIVE BEHAVIOR:

Another great way to avoid your feelings is with compulsive behavior. What do you do when you feel stressed or upset? Some favorite options are cleaning, eating, alcohol, drugs, exercise, or work. This is how many people deal with emotions they do not want to feel. It is a great distraction, and it moves you out of your feelings.

BECOMING A VICTIM:
Blaming others and the world at large is also a popular choice for people when dealing with issues. This moves you into a "poor me" state and takes the responsibility off you. In a victim state, you give away your power and become weak.

ACTING OUT:
This is the method of using other people and situations to create drama or an outburst. A person who acts out uses the outside world to shift the focus off their feelings. These types of people have learned to manipulate energy and others to play their game. By creating drama, the emotion is focused on the outside event.

Your Emotional Operating System has been developed and perfected over many years. You watched your parents, saw what worked, and developed your own system. Once in place, this became the way you process and manage your emotions. Unfortunately, most of us were not given any emotional upgrades.

We are constantly upgrading our computer and cell phone systems. Every time you receive a notice, you quickly update your software. This ensures your device will be working at the highest level. You should be doing the same thing for your Emotional Operating System. Too bad we do not receive a notice to upgrade ourselves.

I have many videos about energy on one of my YouTube Channels: **https://aShotofJoe.com**

The process of upgrading your Emotional Operating System is based on a few key items. First, and most important, is your desire to change and accept that you are creating everything. There can be no blame or judgment here. These feelings move you into victim mode, and there is no power in this state.

As I said earlier, your life reflects your emotional state. When you change your emotional state, you change your life in the physical world. All lasting changes in your life are internal. The external is simply showing you how you are doing on the inside.

The question is . . . how do you upgrade your *Emotional Operating System* and make the positive changes you are truly seeking?

The first thing is stopping yourself and taking a step back before you move into your normal routine. I had this experience a while back when I was first learning about energy principles and emotions. A businessman named Tom had come to see me speak at an event. He asked me if I would be interested in speaking to several groups from his organization in five different cities. We set up a meeting at his office to go over the details.

Everything went well, we agreed on a rate, and he gave me the dates and cities. This was one of the biggest deals I had ever put together at the time. Tom even invited my wife and me to a great event in Manhattan to meet some of his coworkers.

A month later I received an email from Tom telling me the project had been cancelled and they would not be moving forward at this time. My first thought was, wow, a one-sentence email, not even the courtesy of a phone call. In the past I would have been very upset and moved into a deep depression. My usual routine was repressing my feelings and then becoming depressed.

This time I was at a much higher level of awareness. I stopped and allowed myself to move past the initial upset. This led me to the real feeling I was holding, disappointment. This was an episode I realized I had experienced with my father. I had replayed it many times and always became depressed. By allowing myself to feel the emotion, the energy was released.

Upgrading your Emotional Operating System is all about stopping your old patterns and feeling the true emotion. As you would imagine, this takes practice and time to master.

Here are the five steps to help you upgrade:

1 AWARENESS:
When I say awareness, I am not referring to your surroundings. I am referring to your feelings. It is very important to be aware of how you are feeling all day long. Most people run around all day from one task to the next and slide into their unconscious behavior to deal with issues. Now, you want to stop when something upsets you and ask yourself this simple question: "How do I feel?" This simple question will change your life forever.

2 ACCEPTANCE:
Next, you want to accept how you feel without judgment. What does that mean? Your feeling is not good or bad, it simply is what it is. If you feel angry, you must allow yourself to feel that emotion. Do not say or think, "I should not be angry about this." That is a judgment, and it will take you out of your emotion.

3 IDENTIFY WHAT YOU ARE REALLY FEELING:
When dealing with emotions, it is important to truly understand what you are really feeling. You may be feeling angry, for example, but that is just the surface of the deeper emotion. I always ask clients to go under the surface feeling and identify the deeper emotion.

Why are you angry? How is this person or situation making you feel? For example, one of my clients, Judy, was having issues at work. She was always angry at her boss for not acknowledging her ideas. When I asked her about the feeling, she said, "I feel like I do not matter and what I say is not important. It makes me feel unworthy." That is the core emotion that needs to be addressed.

4 FINDING THE EMOTIONAL ANCHOR:
Once you know what the emotion is, unworthiness in this example, you must find out where it started. Who made you feel unworthy

as child? This will usually be tied back to one of your parents or guardians. Judy was able to track this back to her father.

She remembered a specific incident when she finished a science project and was excited to show her father. He was dismissive and made her feel the project was no big deal. Judy was angry with her father, but on a deeper level, she was hurt—she felt unimportant and unworthy.

5 ALLOW YOURSELF TO FEEL THE EMOTION:

When you bring up an incident like this, it is charged with emotion. Most of us have been conditioned to block the feeling in some way. Now you are going to allow yourself to be angry at your father and then feel the unworthiness you have been blocking. You are not necessarily angry at your father. You are upset about how he made you feel. Feel the feeling in a pure sense with no judgment. This emotional exercise releases the negative energy you have been holding.

Every time you allow yourself to feel your emotions without judgment, you are upgrading your Emotional Operating System. Be aware of how you feel and let the emotions flow. You will shift your energy and change your life for the better.

Be aware of how you feel and your reactions. This will help you stop your old behavior and move you to higher ground. Your awareness gives you the opportunity to adjust your Emotional Operating System. All major changes are the result of a series of adjustments. Each change creates new energy and positive momentum. These emotional upgrades will play a major role in your growth and development.

3

BECOMING A HYBRID

CREATING A NEW GENERATION OF HIGH-ENERGY ENTREPRENEURS

What is a hybrid?

hy·brid

Noun

The offspring of two plants or animals of different species or varieties, such as a mule (a hybrid of a donkey and a horse).

As you can see from the definition, it is combining two things that do not necessarily go together to create something new. In this case, it is combining universal spiritual energy principles with entrepreneurship, sales, and business. Our hybrid will become a "High-Energy Entrepreneur."

Traditional logic and history may tell us this is not possible. Many of the powerful, successful people we have seen are not the most magnanimous. These characters have been dominating the landscape for thousands of years. From the ruthless Egyptian Pharaohs and Roman Caesars to Genghis Kahn and Hitler. This list also includes many famous business leaders and politicians who built their empires by abusing others for personal gain, as mentioned earlier.

At first a hybrid may seem strange or off-putting. This also happens when a new technology or philosophy is introduced to the world. Many people fear what is new and automatically resist it. People say they want change, but most are terrified of anything new. I will never forget what happened when computers were introduced into the workplace. When I started my career in sales, there was not much technology to speak of. Our big piece of technology was a pager.

In the mid-nineties, computers started to enter our world in great numbers. Our sales director was in his early fifties at the time. He was an old-school, hard-core sales guy. I remember a meeting where he said, *"These computers are just a fad."* He did not adjust well and as a result was let go.

There are many examples of humans resisting new ideas and technology. Here are just a few:

» Refrigeration
» Coffee
» Electricity
» The Printing Press

Can you imagine not having these things in your life today? All were met with extreme resistance for various reasons. If you are interested in more detail, there is a good book on the topic, titled *Innovation and Its Enemies,* by Calestous Juma.

We are seeing resistance now with artificial intelligence. All innovation has its pluses and minuses. AI will be no different as it develops and becomes more prominent. Self-driving cars and other innovations are scaring people who fear these new ideas. In ten years, we may all be sitting in our self-driving cars wondering how we ever lived without them.

People are also quick to fear and resist new philosophies. This was the case with Jesus, Buddha, and Gandhi, to name a few.

New philosophies are even more personal as they challenge old belief systems with new ideas. I remember having this experience when I started to study energy principles and metaphysics. Many of these concepts ran counter to what I had learned growing up as a Catholic. Reincarnation, no sins, or punishments were just a few of the concepts that were not aligned with what I had learned in Catholic school. It took me a while to truly embrace these new ideas and make peace with them.

Now we are ready to bring a totally new philosophy to the world of business and sales. When I started to talk about Spiritual Selling in 2005, there was a lot of fear and resistance. I still encounter some strange looks and resistance today, but more and more people are ready for this change.

The big question is, why are people so afraid?

The main answer is fear of loss. If I change A, I will lose B. And if I lose B what will happen to me? This is the reason people stay in jobs and relationships that aren't working. The fear of loss is so powerful it causes people to remain in negative situations. They would rather live in the negative than take a chance on a positive change.

Another big issue is fear of the unknown. When you try something new, you are not sure what will happen. Will it work? What will I do if it doesn't work? These are the types of questions that come up in your head as you prepare to try something new.

I always ask clients, what is the best thing that could happen? Then I ask, isn't that worth the risk? Most of the time, people respond with an emphatic YES!

You must believe in what you are doing and stay the course. There are sure to be some bumps in the road, and you want to accept that as part of your journey. Change is never smooth.

When you embrace the concept of "bumps in the road," the transition becomes a lot easier. In energy terms we call it holding the vibration. You must hold that belief and feeling long enough to break through to the other side. Then it will become your new home.

BE A PRO

One of the negative associations with spiritual people is they are flakes. I understand this label especially in the business world. I have encountered so many incredibly talented people who were unable to make a living. They were healers, psychics, mediums, and artists to name a few. This was the result of having no understanding of basic business concepts or the desire to learn.

We are still living in a physical world, and as a result we must be able to operate in this third dimension. This does not mean you have to become an expert in all things business, but you want to know how to operate in an effective manner or hire people to help you.

As we make this change to a new way of operating in the business world, it is important to break through the many misconceptions people are holding. The idea that a spiritually based person cannot be good in business is a myth. This is where the hybrid comes in to play.

I was a businessman first and a spiritualist second. Having a business background gives me credibility with people in the corporate world. That said, they still questioned the concept of Spiritual Selling.

You will fall into one of two categories:
1. You Are More of a Businessperson
2. You Are More of a Spiritual Person

CATEGORY #1: YOU ARE MORE OF A BUSINESSPERSON

As a businessperson you have certain beliefs based on what you learned in your career. Some of these will be good fundamental business principles. Others will run counter to your new spiritual beliefs and feelings.

The key here is blending the two. This is what being a hybrid is all about. I am not giving up one or the other. I am blending the two to create a better version. In this case you decide what to keep and what to remove.

Make a list of your beliefs on both sides. What do you believe you have to do to be successful? What does it mean to be spiritual? We all carry old beliefs in these areas. You probably learned you must work very hard and make huge sacrifices to succeed. Is this true? That is all up to you. There is no true; there is only your perception and belief.

Take your time and be honest regarding your list. This will help you see where you may have some internal conflicts and issues. Be aware of how you feel about these beliefs. Many people I encounter do not face their truth. This creates resistance which slows the process. When people are too insistent, I know they are not dealing with their true beliefs.

If you are still holding a "nose-to-the-grindstone" mentality and belief, accept it. Then, and only then, can you begin to dissolve the energy you are holding. This is the key to removing negative energy and limitations. Acceptance, truth, and removal.

Here is a good exercise to let these negative energies and beliefs go. Begin by making a statement based on something you believe to be true.

1. Example: At this moment I believe I must work very hard and sacrifice to be successful
2. I accept that this is a belief I am holding onto right now
3. I wish to release this belief and move into ease and flow

This is the important part because saying the words is only part of it. Most people get stuck right there because they believe positive affirmations will get them over the hump.

Be aware of how you feel when you say these words. How do you feel when you say each line? Do you really believe it or are you just saying it? Look for the surge in emotion; that will tell you where you are blocked. In the end it is all about faith. You either believe it or you don't. Having true faith takes time, especially when you have not seen the results you desire. This was a major area of struggle and resistance for me. Be patient—as you continue to work on your feelings the fear will dissolve, and your faith will shine through.

CATEGORY #2: YOU ARE MORE OF A SPIRITUAL PERSON

In this case you have a deeper understanding of yourself and the world of energy. People in this category have challenges dealing with the harsh world of business. All you want to do is be yourself, have integrity, and help people. This is great when you are working with people in the same energy. Not so much when you enter the real world.

You will encounter people at all levels. Some of the prospects you meet will not be right for you. Accept this truth and move on to the next one. When you encounter negativity and resistance, it is time to move on.

The other prospects you encounter will be at different levels. As you raise your level of energy, you will attract more people who understand and appreciate what you are offering.

In the beginning you will attract a mixed bag. Some will love you but may not be able to afford what you are offering. Do not lower your rates to accommodate these people. This lowers your energy and ability to receive and prosper. I know you want to help everyone, but you can't do it at your expense.

Create lower level offers for people who cannot afford your time. I offer coaching and consulting at a higher rate. If that is too high, people can get a book or program at a lower price to help them get started.

Use the same exercise outlined for the people in Category #1. What are your feelings and beliefs regarding sales and business?

Here is a good exercise to let these negative energies go:

1. Example: At this moment I believe I am not a good businessperson and cannot build a successful business (or you fear sales and business)
2. I accept that this is a belief I am holding onto right now
3. I wish to release this belief and know I will become a successful business and salesperson

Once again be aware of your feelings, as they will help you uncover your blocks and fears in this area. You have options when it comes to becoming a better businessperson. You can learn to do it yourself or hire people to do some of the tasks. I do some basic accounting, but my accountant handles the heavy lifting.

Gaining a basic understanding of sales and marketing is most important. If you can't sell your product or service, you don't have a business. Selling is the most fun you will ever have when everything is aligned.

4

HELPING IS HEALING

Think of your business as a red Ferrari sitting in your driveway. It is truly a beautiful machine. The Ferrari represents your product or service. It may be the greatest thing in the world but without sales no one will ever know about it. Sales is the fuel needed to drive the Ferrari forward. Without fuel, your gorgeous Ferrari will just sit there collecting dust.

Not all sales are created equally. The quality of your sale, like the quality of the fuel you feed your Ferrari, is very important. A quality sale is high-octane fuel. It makes your engine run more efficiently. Conversely, a low-quality sale erodes your engine from the inside. The interesting thing about a low-quality sale is you do not notice the damage right away. It may in fact look like a better deal in the short term. Over time all those bad deals build up like sludge in your engine. Suddenly the engine ceases and your beautiful Ferrari is finished.

When companies focus on up-front profit above all else, it is sure to have a negative long-term impact on the business. I have seen and experienced this on many occasions. Companies are pushing for sales to drive numbers at the expense of quality and customer satisfaction.

Pay close attention to the quality of your deals. Make sure you create a positive situation for all parties. This may take longer, but in the long run you are building a much stronger business. Anyone can push and manipulate people into buying something. Building a solid, sustainable business takes consistent work, dedication, and patience. In the end it is your ticket to prosperity.

LET THE HEALING BEGIN

Sales have always been viewed as a battle of attrition. When you make the deal, you win, and when you don't, you lose. I have seen many sales managers and trainers criticize salespeople for failing to close a deal. The idea was, they kept their money, and you did not get your commission. This is an extreme concept with no gray area.

Many people in the world of sales and business are playing, what is referred to in economic theory as, a zero-sum game. In this case, one party wins and the other loses. This is the basis of all competitions. The perception or belief that there must be a winner and a loser in every transaction. If you believe you must win to be successful, you will never be able to help someone heal.

I always start sessions with this question . . . What is a sale? Stop for a moment and write down your definition of a sale. Then sit with it and see how it feels.

I watched a show about Henry Heinz; you know, the catsup guy. He was the first person to sell his product in a clear bottle to show purity and quality. Prior to that, the quality of condiments was not very good, and manufacturers used dark-colored bottles to hide the less-than-stellar quality. He found out that one of his competitors wanted to use the same bottles, so Heinz purchased all the clear bottles, even though he could not use them. He sent them out on a barge and sunk them in the ocean, not allowing the competitor to use them. That is a zero-sum game for sure.

The idea that there is not enough to go around has created feelings of lack and fear. These are negative feelings, and people act accordingly to protect their interests. If I believe it is necessary to win to succeed, that is where I focus my attention. In this case, you are not working from a pure space. You are more concerned with winning than doing something positive for all parties.

In higher awareness we are playing a non-zero-sum game. In this case, everyone wins. The concept here is, how do we create a situation where both parties feel good about the transaction. Let's say you and I both own restaurants. I have extra chicken and you have too much fish. We trade with each other, and everyone wins.

Has anyone ever told you that you helped someone heal by making a sale? At a higher level, when you create a quality transaction you are helping someone heal. Those of us working from a higher perspective understand that fact. Every time I sign a new client, sell a book or program, I know healing has occurred.

Let's get back to the question, what is a sale?

At a higher level, a sale is an **exchange of energy**.

A transaction has taken place on two levels. On a physical level there has been an exchange of money for a product or service. On an emotional level there has been an exchange of energy. The question is, how do both parties feel when the transaction is complete?

In a non-zero-sum game, both parties walk away feeling they have made a fair deal. There is no feeling of loss. This should be your goal when you are transacting business. It is important to remember that both parties feel good. Giving away too much or creating an imbalanced deal is not the goal. The more aware you are, the easier this will be.

WHAT IS YOUR INTENTION?

Your energy works on the premise of focus and expansion. What you focus on, and feel is what you create. Your intention is an important part of this process. You must remember that energy is non-judgmental. It is not good or bad. If your desire is to succeed at all costs, that is the intention. Rockefeller, Vanderbilt, and

Carnegie had this intention and were very successful. Do you feel this makes them bad people? As I mentioned earlier, there is no need to judge others.

The key is your intention. It makes no difference what others are doing. In many cases we are focused on and comparing ourselves to others, which is a terrible idea. You are the center of your world. Keep that thought at the top of your awareness all day.

Pure intention is tied to your desire to create, share, and help others. In this space, you are focused on the joy of creating something that will benefit others and yourself. Remember, you are one of the people who benefits. This is also something to remain focused on. Many are trapped in a belief that it is all about giving and not receiving. The universe seeks balance. We are not here to be self-sacrificing martyrs. We are here to create, heal, and love.

YOUR JOB IS TO SERVE

In the end, we are all here to be of service and share our gifts with the world. I know that seems so simple to say. Part of the struggle we all face is based on the emotional journey we are here to experience. We need the pain and failure to truly experience the joy of breaking through.

Focus your energy on serving people and making their lives better. Not just by offering a great product or service but by sharing your love and positive energy with every person you touch. There are many cases when I walk away without a deal in the physical world. On a deeper level, I know I left that person with new positive energy that will help in their journey.

Having this feeling goes against core business principles. Why would I want to send good energy to a person who did not buy from me? Because that is why I am here. To be a light for everyone. Every time you send good energy, you are elevated. Your positive energy will help someone move their life forward. You will be rewarded for your kindness in the future. Think of it as building your bank of good vibes.

The one thing to be aware of is overextending yourself. This is a trap many spiritual people fall into. You may feel guilty at first, and this is a feeling you will have to address. I receive many emails and calls from people asking for help. If I tried to answer all of them, I would be exhausted and drained. Know your limits, set boundaries, and deal with the emotions as they come up. This is all part of your journey to higher energy and balance.

Your negative ego wants immediate gratification and keeps score of each encounter. Your higher self knows you are being guided along the perfect path for your highest and greatest good. Your good vibes will be rewarded when the time is right for you to receive. Trust the universe and know you are here to give and receive.

You are here to . . .

Serve

Share

&

Prosper

Always keep those three things in front of you and live in that space. Your focus creates energy, your energy creates vibration, and your vibration attracts what you desire.

Keep Healing Others and Watch Yourself Soar to New Levels of Success!

5

HOW I BECAME
SPIRITUAL

I gained my spirituality later in life and feel it is important to share my experience to create context for this process. Many people ask me how and why I developed the concept of Spiritual Selling. For this reason, I felt it was important to share my experience. Each person takes their own unique journey in the quest to gain peace and enlightenment. My journey was completely unexpected and filled with many twists and turns.

Both sides of my family are originally from Brooklyn, New York. I was born and raised in Brooklyn until the age of seven, at which time we moved to Queens, seeking greener pastures. For those of you not from New York, moving from the concrete-ridden streets of Brooklyn to a neighborhood filled with small, green patches of grass is considered quite the upgrade.

We lived a simple middle-class life and moved to an even better part of Queens when I was nine. My father was a New York City police officer on the fast track. He started as a *Mountie*, the term used for a cop who rode a horse through the streets of the city.

Later he would become a detective in Manhattan.

My father, for whom I am named, was a very dynamic person to say the least. He was gregarious, well liked, and handsome. As his career progressed, he was promoted to an elite narcotics unit in New York City. The demands of his job and his desire to succeed did not leave much time for family. My mother, younger sister, and I ate dinner without him almost every night. We were accustomed to not having him around, so we adjusted.

All things were quite normal until March 27, 1972. On that day I was walking home from school, as I did every day, with my friend Mike Olivieri. We stopped in my driveway to flip a few baseball cards before going in to do homework. Our house had a long driveway with the garage in the back. We always used the side door, which led into the kitchen, as the main entrance. The weather was beginning to warm up, and we enjoyed staying outside in the bright sunshine.

Suddenly the side door swung open, and my grandfather appeared. He usually only came over on the weekend, and I was surprised to see him in the middle of the week. In addition, he was smoking a cigarette, something I had never seen him do. I was happy to see him, so these oddities were not something that I gave much attention to at the time. "Hey, Gramp, what are you doing here?" I cried out. He looked at me with piercing eyes and said, "Come inside, Joey," in a stern voice. Although all these things were out of character, none of them had any effect on me.

I walked into the house and immediately knew something was wrong. There were people everywhere and a sense of chaos pervaded. I seemed to glide through the kitchen into the living room. My mother grabbed me and pressed me against her chest. "Daddy went to heaven today," she sighed. At that moment the entire room seemed to be moving in slow motion.

My father had died of a bullet wound to the chest that morning. The shot was fired by his own gun and the death was immediately ruled a suicide. Shortly after the incident, evidence was discovered that shed doubt on the actual cause of death. Questions began to arise, but most were quickly covered up. The bullet entered just under the left armpit. My father was left-handed, and this would have been an almost impossible angle for him to fire his weapon. There were no powder burns on his hands, and any that may have been on his clothes, which could have proven the distance of the gun from his body, vanished mysteriously.

The New York City Police Department denied my mother his pension because the death was deemed a suicide. After years in court, my mother walked away without a single dime from the police department. There she was, a thirty-seven-year-old woman with two children, no husband, and no pension. Life for us would never be the same.

We all went on with our lives, but the mystery surrounding the events of my father's death would haunt me for the next twenty-five years. The event affected each person in the family in a different way. I went from being an excellent student to being a person who had totally lost interest in school. All I wanted to do was finish high school and start working. I attended a Catholic high school for three years, then transferred to a public school for my senior year.

I had a revelation growing up that changed the direction of my life. As a kid I began to realize that all the people we knew who were successful either owned businesses or were involved in selling something. Why should I waste my time in college when the real money was in the business world? In my eyes, the faster I started, the faster I would achieve the success I desired.

My career began immediately following graduation. I started working on a truck delivering Budweiser beer in Brooklyn. The company was owned by a family friend who had grown up with my mother. I was thrilled to be out of school and earning money on my own.

Within a year, I had my sights set on bigger opportunities. I had saved some money and was now ready to start my own business.

At nineteen years old, I felt it was time for me to start building my own empire. A few months later, I purchased my first business, a soda route, in Brooklyn. My mother co-signed a loan for me to get started, and off I went.

Owning a route gives you the exclusive right to distribute certain products in a specific territory. My main product was YooHoo chocolate drinks. The neighborhood I selected was the Crown Heights/Bedford-Stuyvesant section of Brooklyn. This was one of the most dangerous neighborhoods in the city. I was so excited to be buying the business that I did not see the danger lurking around every corner. This was a reality that I would learn about in short order.

The first few weeks were great as the former owner rode with me and showed me the ropes. It was the beginning of the summer and the soda business was thriving. I made more money in the first few weeks than I had ever seen before in my life. Times were good, and I felt I was on my way to fulfilling my dreams.

Those dreams were quickly shattered over the next few months as I was held up at knifepoint and gunpoint. I was robbed and left standing in the middle of the street, trembling. I realized that in an instant my life could be over on these unforgiving streets. Each morning as I woke, a feeling of fear enveloped my body. Every delivery seemed to be filled with the possibility of danger and incident. I approached each day with trepidation and hoped I had enough courage to hold on and keep the business going.

A COP COMES TO MY AID

One day a young police officer approached my truck. He saw a young kid alone in a treacherous neighborhood as a sitting duck. The officer was a tall, strapping guy in his neatly pressed uniform complete with dazzling badge. "How are you doing, kid?" he queried.

"Not too bad," I replied.

"Have you had any trouble out here?" he asked.

I explained how I had been robbed twice and that I was feeling a bit nervous. He told me to wait a minute as he went to his squad car. The officer—I will call him Officer Jones—returned with a piece of paper that he pressed into my hand. "Go see this guy and tell him I sent you," he explained.

The piece of paper contained an address and a name, *Jamaican Pete*. I was told to ask for him and he would help me. The next day I drove my inconspicuous soda truck down Flatbush Avenue to the address on the paper. When I arrived there, I was surprised to see that it was a butcher shop. I walked into the rustic-looking store, complete with sawdust on the floor and large meat scale in the middle of the counter.

I proceeded to tell the guy behind the counter that I was sent by Officer Jones, and I was looking for Jamaican Pete. A few minutes later a diminutive man sauntered out of the back room, wearing a pair of bamboo sandals and a white butcher's coat and sporting a head full of dreadlocks. He told me to follow him to the back of the store. He took me to a huge steel door with a giant bolt lock. Jamaican Pete opened the door and invited me into the next room. Then he proceeded to lock the door behind him. To say I was nervous would not begin to explain the feelings that were running through my veins. My first thought was, *I'm Italian—I know how these things work.*

Once we were inside, he moved to the other end of the small room where a wooden cabinet covered the entire back wall. He pulled open the cabinet door, exposing a wall of guns. As it turned out, Jamaican Pete was selling illegal guns in the back of his shop, and a cop had sent me there. A more bizarre set of conditions I could not fathom.

"So, you're out there trying to work, and those punks are giving you trouble," he said with a disgusted tone. I explained how I had been robbed and involved in several street altercations. "Okay, this is what we are going to do to take care of your problem. First, I am going to give you a .22 automatic to keep in your pants. Make sure when you walk around everyone can see it. Then I am going to give you a small .22 revolver to keep on your ankle just in case." *Wow, buy one, get one free*, I thought. I left the store in a state of complete confusion and shock at what had just transpired.

In what seemed like an instant, the weather began to turn cold, and business slowed dramatically. Within a year I was out of business and forced to declare bankruptcy. I was only twenty years old at the time. This failure had a devastating effect on my self-esteem and confidence.

There was no time to feel sorry for myself. I had to pay back the loan my mother had co-signed, and the bank was not interested in my problems. Without much thought I decided to become a bartender. I knew some guys who were making good money and it was cash. The drinking age in New York was eighteen at the time, so my age was not an issue.

A few weeks later I was standing behind a bar in Manhattan. Over the next five years, I worked in several nightclubs and bars. Eventually I landed in a club in lower Manhattan and was promoted to manager. I found an apartment in the neighborhood and felt like I was back on track. The money I made allowed me to pay off the loan to the bank and relieve some of my feelings of guilt and failure.

One dark morning I was standing on Bleecker Street in the Greenwich Village section of the city. It was 5:00 A.M. I had just finished work, and the streets were filled with people who had been a part of the evening's festivities. The block was lined with a series of bars and clubs. This was an eclectic group that included musicians, singers, artists, comedians, actors, and of course staff members of all these establishments. Many of us would go out for coffee or hit an after-hours club after work to unwind.

On this early morning, I took stock in myself and the future. I was twenty-five years old, and the friends I had laughed at for going to college were now forging careers and starting 401(k) plans. I was living week to week and had no idea where my life was heading.

I decided it was time to go out and look for a real job. To this day I am not sure what the term *real job* actually means. On my way home from work, I picked up a copy of the Sunday *New York Times*. This was the bible of job-searching tools at the time, before the Internet changed the landscape. I woke up early on Sunday and sat there leafing through the paper with my red pen. As I turned the pages, I quickly realized I had no idea what I was looking for in this sea of ink and words.

In most cases I did not understand the job descriptions or positions being offered. Another issue was the common requirement of a college degree, which I did not possess. My lack of education was another internal battle I would fight for many years. Just as my frustration reached its limit, I arrived in the sales section at the back of the paper. These jobs seemed to be completely different. As the ads all seemed to say, "If you are breathing, we would love to see you."

I proceeded to go to four interviews and to my amazement was offered a job each time. Later I realized that *everyone* received an offer because these were straight commission jobs, and you were only paid if you sold something. I had no other options, so I selected a job selling advertising space in a local publication. This was a strange new world for me. There was structure, reports, meetings, and paperwork. I was used to the fast and loose nightclub world, which was devoid of any such inconvenience.

Sales felt very natural to me right from the start. I was comfortable speaking to strangers, a skill I acquired as a bartender, and making them feel comfortable. Within a few months I was one of the top salespeople in my division and was soon training others. I went on to learn as much as I could about copywriting, a key skill in the ad sales market.

After about a year, I started to look for a better opportunity. I met someone in the direct mail business and started to sell coupon mailing packages. This was my first exposure to the direct response industry. A year later I started my own direct mail marketing business. This time I was determined not to make the same mistakes I had made in my failed soda delivery business.

The business was inconsistent from the start and continued that way for the next few years. I would have great success for a period and then go into very slow periods with very little money coming in. I will spare you the gory details, but after a few years I was forced into a second bankruptcy. Now I was a twice-bankrupt entrepreneur by the age of thirty. All of my dreams and visions had been replaced with feelings of utter frustration. In addition to the frustration, I was extremely confused and disappointed. I could not comprehend how all of my hard work and dedication had produced such failure. This bankruptcy came a few months after I was married. Not the best way to start a new life with someone.

A LIGHT AT THE END OF THE TUNNEL

A few years before my second bankruptcy—October 2, 1987, to be exact—I had met the most important person in my life. I was in a Manhattan nightclub with a group of friends when Marie D'Angelo came into my life. I did not realize it at the time, but this amazing woman would later become my wife, best friend, and biggest supporter and would introduce me to the world of spirituality. I was a hard-core worker, a no-excuses, get-the-job-done type of guy. All this esoteric spiritual talk was not something I could relate to in my current condition.

Shortly before my second bankruptcy, I had begun going to therapy. Unfortunately, it was not soon enough to save my direct mail business. I went for a few years, gaining clarity and a much deeper understanding of what was happening in my life. Now I was ready to move to a higher level of awareness. This led me to the exploration of spiritual and universal laws.

I started a new job selling advertising space for another company. We were struggling financially, and I was very unhappy with my job. Then, one rainy Saturday in the fall of 1991, my life changed again. Marie had gone out to visit a relative at the hospital and I was home alone for the day. We lived in an apartment in the Whitestone section of Queens at the time. I remember feeling depressed about my job and a general lack of enthusiasm about my life.

The rain was teeming down so it was a perfect day to lounge around and watch a good movie. I was flipping around the dial when I came upon a PBS special featuring John Bradshaw. He had a new book out called *Homecoming* and was one of the original people to speak about the inner child. He was on for the entire day, and I found myself mesmerized by his message. I sat there entranced like a four-year-old watching *Barney*. He spoke about inner pain and how those feelings create different problems in our lives.

Marie returned to find me in the same position she had left me in hours before. I couldn't wait to tell her all about this amazing man and his message. The next day I ran out to buy his book and started the next step in my journey.

After watching the show and reading the book, I felt connected to this work. I knew, on an internal level, that I would one day do something similar with my life. In September 1992, I started my current business, Top Notch Training, a training and seminar company. I had absolutely no idea how to do it. The one thing I knew for sure was that I had to do it. I kept my job in ad sales and started to work on the seminar business on a part-time basis. This would be my life for the next eight-plus years.

My corporate career went well as I continued to receive promotions and increases in pay. However, although I did a good job and was productive, my heart was always in my teaching work. I had become a little more open to spirituality, but I was still working in more of a psychological capacity. I continued to study and began offering some local seminars. I would speak anywhere an opportunity would arise. I knew I had to get out there and start to practice my new profession.

ENTER JOHN EDWARD

You may know of John Edward from his television show *Crossing Over* or from one of his many books about speaking with people who have, in his terms, crossed over. He is a medium, someone who contacts the dead. In 1997 he was a little-known psychic/medium on Long Island. I did not know much about him at the time.

On February 19, 1997, I was working for a local cable company selling television spots. I was always out in my car driving around Long Island, seeing clients. Late that morning I received a call on my cell phone from my wife. One of her friends had made an appointment to see John Edward and could not make it. Even at that time it was extremely difficult to get an appointment. People could only call one day a month to schedule time with him.

The appointment was scheduled for 4:30 that afternoon. Marie thought it was a good idea for me to go, as this opportunity had seemed to come for a reason. I agreed to go and went about my business for the rest of the day. It was a busy day, and I did not spend much time thinking about this meeting. I arrived without any real expectations for the session.

Following the directions, I pulled up to a simple house located on a cul-de-sac in the Huntington section of Long Island. I walked up to the door and rang the bell. I had no idea what John Edward looked like, and a part of me was expecting someone reminiscent of Merlin the magician. To my great surprise, a man in his early thirties opened the door to greet me. He was wearing jeans and a white T-shirt. John Edward looked like a regular guy you would see at the supermarket. There was a look of surprise on his face, as the appointment was originally made for a woman. I explained how she was unable to come and that I was taking her place. He asked me for my first name only.

We proceeded upstairs to begin the session. I was still expecting something weird to happen at some point. Maybe this room would be bathed in red light and filled with smoke. Once again, I was surprised to enter what was a very normal looking home office. There was a desk in the middle of a small room. He sat behind the desk and invited me to sit on the opposite side. This felt more like a business meeting than a psychic experience.

I was then given a basic outline of what was about to happen. John told me he does not have any control over who comes through. He explained a few terms he would be using; *above* meant the person was older than me, *to the side* indicated they were around the same age, and *below* meant they were younger. Another important instruction was not to try to make something fit that did not make sense.

The session went like this, to the best of my recollection:

JOHN: May I have something of yours to hold?

JOE: Take my wedding band.

He started to rub my ring in his right hand.

JOHN: I have Joseph. Who is that?

JOE: That is my father.

JOHN: He looks like you but his face is a little wider and he is a bit stockier.

JOE: That is a pretty good description.

JOHN: He is showing me a badge. Was he a cop?

JOE: Yes.

JOHN: He is telling me he did not wear a uniform. I see him wearing a long, camel hair coat.

JOE: Yes, he was a detective, and he loved that coat.

Note: I am starting to get freaked out.

JOHN: He died outside.

JOE: Yes, he did.

JOHN. Did he die in front of his house? He is telling me this is a very familiar place.

JOE: He was found in his unmarked car in Brooklyn a few blocks from where he grew up.

JOHN: I do not mean to be disrespectful, but was he involved with the Mafia in any way?

JOE: That is very possible.

JOHN: He knows the people who did it. He let them into the back of the car. I see a lot of blood.

JOE: The death was originally deemed a suicide.

JOHN: No, no, he was murdered.

JOE: Who were these people?

JOHN: I can't tell you that, but he knows them. By the way, did you just add electrical outlets in your bedroom?

JOE: What?

JOHN: That is a validation from him. He wants you to know he's around.

JOE: As a matter of fact, the electrician was over last week adding outlets.

JOHN: He is telling me you have a picture of him wearing a uniform.

JOE: We have one when he was young in his police uniform.

JOHN: No, not that one.

JOE: We have another of him in a baseball uniform. He played minor league baseball.

JOHN: No, not that one.

JOE: I can't think of another one we have.

JOHN: He is showing a little boy wearing a sailor suit.

JOE: Oh boy, we have an old family portrait of his oldest brother getting married.

My father was the youngest of twelve. He was around eight years old at the time of that photo, and he is wearing a sailor suit. We have that photo displayed in our den.

To say I was blown away when I left would be the understatement of the year. I sat in my car for half an hour after the session to collect myself. This was one of the most incredible experiences of my life. It seemed to happen in rapid-fire succession and be over in one minute. The session lasted forty minutes.

We discussed several other issues that day. John talked about my wedding, the birth of my son, and about my mother and sister. He expressed my father's feelings and told me my father wanted me to know he was there for all of it. I had been hoping to gain some closure on my father's death, and for the first time in twenty-five years, I was at peace with the incident. A feeling of tranquility came over me that day.

This incredible experience has had a lasting effect on my life. I left there knowing that there were things happening in the universe beyond my wildest imagination. Although I had previously been exposed to some of these concepts and ideas, my session with John Edward proved to be a trigger point for me. I dove into spiritual teachings and training headfirst. My entry into the world of spirituality had truly begun.

ON MY OWN

In December 2001, I was asked to leave my job as the national sales director of a London-based Internet fashion forecasting service. I was running the US office from New York City at the time. The volatile owner of the company and his ego-driven sales director did not see eye to eye on many issues.

This was two months after 9/11, and New York City was in a state of recovery. I will never forget the feeling of riding on the Long Island Railroad into Manhattan each day. This usually bustling train was transformed into a memorial service on wheels. On a normal morning people would be chatting, playing cards, watching movies on their laptops, or reading the morning paper. In the weeks that followed 9/11, the entire train was completely silent for the length of the trip.

People sat quietly as we all felt a connection to the events of that awful day. It was a time of change for all of us. The entire city had taken on a new persona, and I was glad to be moving on, especially at that time.

The company owed me severance and other monies upon my departure. I had a few clients lined up and, after a discussion with

Marie, decided it was time to go out on my own. I had recently released my first book, *No More 9 to 5*, a blueprint for starting a business from home, and I was ready to start. In the beginning I did several different things, including business consulting, seminars, and training.

My first year was moving along very well until I lost my biggest client right before the holidays. Things started to fall apart, and all my old demons started to awaken. The feelings of fear I had experienced during my first two bankruptcies were reemerging. This was the beginning of a transitional period that would move me to another level in my life.

I was now immersed in the study of energy and universal laws. This was fascinating to me, and I became transfixed on this topic. Business was sporadic, and I found myself dealing with a series of feelings at the time. I was beginning to understand my feeling of fear, but it would take several more years to resolve most of it. You never truly resolve or release these feelings 100 percent, but we can release significant portions and make dramatic changes.

One night I was browsing Amazon, searching for books on the topic of energy. I looked at a series of different titles, then decided to buy a book called *The System for Soul Memory* by Susan Kerr. For some reason I was drawn to this book even though I had never heard of it or of the author. This amazing book and its author turned out to be pivotal in my life. The book focuses on how the energy we are holding in our bodies creates a vibration that creates our reality. It went on to explain how we hold energy in our *chakras* (energy points in our bodies) that must be cleared to change our internal vibration. I will discuss chakras in more detail later in this book. I had no idea what a chakra was, but it all seemed to make sense to me. I read the book and began to apply some of the principles.

A few months later, my wife had laser surgery to relieve pain in her lower back due to a herniated disc. She felt fine for a while and then started to feel extreme pain. A week later Marie was in the hospital due to a staph infection she picked up after the surgery. She spent two weeks in the hospital and many months recovering at home. It would be more than a year before she would return to full strength. When an event like this happens, all of your priorities are reassessed. The things you thought were so important suddenly become insignificant whispers.

I worked on and off during the year when Marie was recovering. Although I tried to be at my best, I was not focused, and it affected my business greatly. As Marie's condition improved, I started to get back on track with the business. I had lost a lot of momentum and was desperate to rebuild my sales. One day I was sitting in my home office when I saw *The System for Soul Memory,* which I had read a year earlier. As I leafed through the pages, I came upon the author's bio at the back of the book. Susan Kerr was living on Long Island about twenty minutes from me. I decided to send her an e-mail to find out if she had private sessions. We spoke a few days later and made an appointment.

THE APPOINTMENT OF A LIFETIME

Susan Kerr is a psychic and medium and also reads chakra energy. I did not realize the extent of her gifts until we met in person. The address she gave was a building on the South Shore of Long Island's Nassau County. Unlike the John Edward encounter, this session took place in an office building. At first blush it appeared to be more corporate than mystical.

I rode the elevator up and entered a small, rectangular office. I noticed a club chair, coffee table, and sofa as I entered. A desk was positioned at the back of the office in front of a large window. Susan was sitting in a chair behind the desk when I entered. She spun around in her chair and said, "Tony?" I was taken aback for a moment and then replied, "No, I'm Joe." My first thought was, what kind of psychic is this? She didn't even know my name, and she knew I was coming.

Susan hesitated for a moment and then explained how she

was in a transcendent state when I arrived. "Tony is the person who brought you here," she explained. She asked me who was the Tony in my life, and I told her that was the name of my grandfather who had passed a few years earlier. Susan had succeeded in getting my full attention before we began our session.

I took a seat on the sofa, and she sat across from me on the club chair. Within the first three minutes, Susan told me she would be my last teacher. She went on to explain how she was going to teach me how to clear negative energy in the chakras. Then she told me I was going to take this work to a large audience. At this point my head was sizzling at the notion of teaching people how to clear negative energy in their chakras. I didn't really know what a chakra was, and now I was going to help people clear negative energy? I was filled with trepidation about this new course of action I was supposed to take in my life.

We spoke for the next three hours. Susan explained how the chakra energy we are holding inside is the key to success. She told me I was not receiving what I wanted because I had blocks in my chakras and as a result was holding a negative energy vibration. My assignment was to learn how to clear my own negative energy. Once I complete this transformation, I would have the ability to teach others the same process.

This work is based on clearing negative energy from its emotional core. To accomplish this, it would be necessary to connect to deep unconscious feelings that had been repressed for years.

Over the next eighteen months, I went on a journey like no other. I had no idea what to expect but on some innate level knew it was something I had to accomplish in my life. As I started to crack my emotional shell, more and more of my deep-seated feelings were released. I often tell people how I cried every day for more than a year as I released the layers of painful feelings I was carrying.

Like all great achievements in life, this was a long process that required commitment and discipline. Unlike many of the things we have learned in this linear world, this was an organic process. As human beings, we like things that have a beginning, middle, and end. This work is completely different, as it becomes a way of life, as opposed to a static accomplishment that is defined with a diploma or trophy.

The most challenging aspect of this transformation was integrating these new philosophies while attempting to function normally. Had I gone to a mountain cabin and lived alone for a year to deal with my thoughts and feelings, the process would have been much easier. I had no such option in my life. I was running a business, speaking at events, coaching clients, and writing. In addition, I am the husband and father of a wonderful son. My family has always been my number one priority and it always remains paramount in my life.

One of the key elements in my ability to make this transformation was the endorsement of my wife. Marie's support and understanding proved to be the most important element in the process. We did the work together and moved our relationship to a new level of emotional synchronicity.

As time passed, my ability to live a spiritual life became congruent with the rest of my activities. With each passing day I was gaining a greater level of comfort with this completely new way of experiencing life. I started to share these new experiences and techniques with others. As people applied these principles, their lives were transformed forever. I knew I was ready to start spreading the word to a larger audience.

COMING OUT OF THE CLOSET

Although my newfound spirituality was now fully integrated into my life and the lives of my family, I was still positioning myself as a sales and marketing expert. Now it was time to tell the world about my new mission. I was not sure how to get started, but I knew the universe would open the right doors when the time was right.

One of the people I was sharing this information with was Ellen Volpe, a friend who owns a large networking business on Long Island. One day we were talking, and she thought it would be a great idea if I did a presentation on this topic. She offered to plan an event and take care of everything. All I had to do was show up and deliver the presentation. As I said, the universe is always there to help.

I was working on a new program called "No More Mental Barriers." This program was designed to help people break destructive patterns of behavior by clearing their internal negative energy. My plan was to use this program as the basis for my one-hour presentation. The event was scheduled for March 10, 2005, giving me almost three months to prepare myself. I knew that several people in attendance would be shocked to hear me deliver this new material.

The presentation was to begin at eight in the morning. I woke up early after a very restless night in bed. I arrived at the venue and walked around the empty ballroom. Within the hour this room would be filled with over 200 hard-core New York businesspeople. Other than a sip of water, I had not consumed anything that morning. My stomach was bubbling with volcanic activity, and eating was not an option.

Suddenly the room was filled, and it was my time to speak. I remember feeling a wave of emotion just before I started. At one point I felt as if I were watching myself deliver this alien presentation. When I was finished, I felt like a major burden had been lifted. My presentation and new persona were well received, for the most part, and I was on my way into this new work as a spiritual teacher and healer.

One of my objectives was to integrate these spiritual principles with today's business practices. This will create a completely new paradigm for sales and business. This new wave of consciousness has already begun, and we are on the cusp of an exciting new world.

6

THE POWER OF YOUR CHAKRAS

The word *chakra* is an Indian Sanskrit word that means "wheel" or "spiral." Chakras are basically subtle energy channels that run through the body. There are seven main chakras that make up the classical or basic chakra system. I will introduce you to a very powerful eighth chakra as well.

The vibration you send out to the universe is based on the energy you are holding in your chakras. To make long-term changes, you must clear the negative energy you are holding inside. This is accomplished when you release these feelings at their core.

Our society has always been focused on the effect instead of the cause. If you are not making enough sales, then you work harder. If you are overweight, you should change your diet or go to the gym. Most people do not look to the cause—they only see the effect. When you focus only on the effect, you are forever trapped in a cycle of behavior. This is the result of approaching the issue from the outside.

Dealing with the cause revolves around exploring the issue

from the inside. When you are looking at the cause, you are focusing on *why* certain things are occurring in your life. Your experiences are the result of your internal beliefs and the energy vibration emanating from you.

Your chakras develop as you mature, and each one is associated with an area of your body. That is why you may experience emotion as a feeling or sensation in a certain part of your body. The saying, "I have a gut feeling," describes the sensation in your solar plexus chakra, for example. All your chakra development occurs from conception until the age of approximately nine years old, depending on the individual. This development becomes your internal emotional mapping system. All of your feelings, beliefs, patterns, memories, and emotions are stored in the chakras. Everything that has happened in your life began as unconscious energy that manifested in your physical reality. You are always creating your own reality, and only you can change it.

External change occurs when you make internal changes in your energy. These shifts of energy begin to send a different vibration out to the universe. A different vibration will always yield a new result. Each time you release negative energy, you elevate your vibrational frequency. When you are consistently clearing your bad energy, you can't help but attract more positive situations and people into your life.

Your chakras develop from your base and move upward. Think of yourself as a giant sponge. Your chakras and unconscious mind absorb every feeling, emotion, and memory that happens in your life. The fact that you don't remember an occurrence does not mean it has left you. You were absorbing feelings before you were born, and you have never stopped. All these emotions and memories are stored in the chakras. Your problems are based on blocks in the different chakra areas.

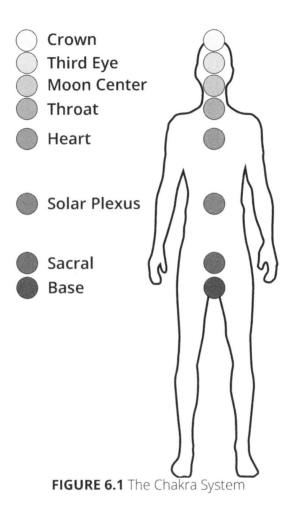

FIGURE 6.1 The Chakra System

Figure 6.1 shows the location of the seven basic chakras plus the moon center chakra in the body.

Base Chakra

Beginning at the bottom, the *base* or *root chakra* begins to develop from conception to age one. All feelings and incidents that occur during this time are stored in this chakra. The base or root chakra is your foundation and is the most powerful. Most of your deep-

rooted, long-term problems stem from here. This is also the chakra that has the greatest effect on your personal sense of worth and self-esteem.
Location: Base of the spine.
Issues include: Work, career, money, and safety issues.

Sacral Chakra
The *sacral chakra* develops in the second year of life. All feelings and incidents that occur during this time are stored in this chakra. At this point the baby becomes aware of the outside world and the needs of others.
Location: Pelvic area.
Issues include: Codependency, blaming others, and feeling lonely (not getting enough attention).

Solar Plexus Chakra
The *solar plexus chakra* develops during the third year of life. All feelings and incidents that occur during this time are stored in this chakra. When a baby reaches the age of three, it begins to explore the world. This chakra determines how powerful you will feel later in life. This is also where you hold you Chi or power.
Location: Navel area.
Issues include: Anger, hopelessness, despair, feeling powerless, and depression.

Heart Chakra
The *heart chakra* develops during the age of four. All feelings and incidents that occur during this time are stored in this chakra. The issues related to the feeling of love and relationships are centered here.
Location: Heart, upper chest.
Issues include: Self-love, compassion, gratitude, mistrust, rejection, and lack of joy.

Throat Chakra

The *throat chakra* develops during the age of five. All feelings and incidents that occur during this time are stored in this chakra. Your ability to communicate and express yourself to others develops at this time.

Location: Throat.

Issues include: Morality, being good or bad, jealousy, seeking approval, and feeling misunderstood.

Moon Center Chakra

The *moon center chakra* develops during your sixth year of life. This little-known chakra holds great power, as it is where you take your first breath.

Location: Nose and Mouth.

Issues include: The feeling of shame, being responsible or not responsible, self-judgment, guilt, and feeling empowered.

Third Eye Chakra

The *third eye chakra* develops during the age of seven. All feelings and incidents that occur during this time are stored in this chakra. Your intuition and psychic ability are developed at this time. Your vision of the world is based on your beliefs and how you interpret them. This chakra determines how you relate to society and the world around you.

Location: Brow.

Issues include: Determination, pride, obsession, conceit, and stubbornness.

Crown Chakra

The *crown chakra* develops during the eighth year. All feelings and incidents that occur during this time period are stored in this chakra. In this area we deal with issues relating to self-truth. The crown chakra is the gateway to your soul. This is where you receive divine guidance and experience love and intense joy.

Location: Top of the head.
Issues include: The feeling of doubt or feeling like a phony. Feelings of joy, acceptance, and being validated.

The chakras are all connected, and your internal energy is always moving through your body. Any disruption or block will cause a disturbance in your flow of energy. These blocks are then manifested in your life in a number of different ways. They affect all areas of your life, including intimate relationships, career, finances, health, and friendships. A long-term change in any area of your life will come only when you have cleared the negative energy in the chakra connected to that feeling.

CLEARING THE CHAKRAS

There are many layers of feelings in each chakra. The deeper the issue, the more layers there will be to clear. Some of your minor issues may be cleared in a relatively short period of time, but your major issues will always be with you on some level. These deeply rooted feelings are extraordinarily difficult to clear completely in one lifetime. Few people have reached a level of enlightenment in this world. However, this does not mean you cannot clear a large portion of these painful feelings and live a very happy life.

Each block is connected to an unconscious feelings of guilt, shame and, fear. These feelings must be released in order to stop the internal desire to re-create pain in your life. As these feelings are released, your internal vibration will be changed.

The desire to create pain in your life is not conscious. That is why it is so difficult to identify and clear these blocks.

I went through two bankruptcies by age thirty because I did not feel I deserved to have money and be successful. This went back to a feeling I was carrying from childhood. I was consciously doing all the things I thought would bring me success. The conscious action I took was sound, but it did not matter because I was carrying the feelings of a person who did not deserve success.

This disconnection of feeling prevented me from receiving the success I desired.

The emotional motivation for my distress was connected to my desire to feel sorry for myself. I had never released the pain I experienced when my father passed. As a result, I unconsciously re-created the feeling. Because I had not grieved this loss and released the feeling, it was still present in my chakras. Struggling financially allowed me to relive the feeling over and over again. It continued to come back because I had never released this energy. If energy is not released, it continues to cycle through your body. Repressed energy is the reason people continue to repeat destructive patterns of behavior.

There is also an emotional benefit attached to this behavior. In my case I received sympathy from others. People would feel sorry for me because I was working so hard and still struggling. This is the emotional payoff that many people become addicted to in their lives. In some cases, it helps them get the attention they craved as children.

The best way I have found to clear negative chakra energy is through emotional release. The key to this release is to move yourself into a state of total truth about the issues in your life. Most of your unconscious negative energy will be attached to the feelings you are holding toward your parents. The energy will be in the form of guilt, shame, and fear. You must realize that this exercise has nothing to do with judging your parents. The key to a successful release revolves simply around your ability to feel the emotions you are repressing.

John always told me his father was the greatest guy you could ever meet. "He was a great provider—he worked hard and provided us with a very comfortable lifestyle," John proclaimed. He had always described his father as a good provider. One day I started to ask him more questions about their relationship. "How did he make you feel when you spent time together?" I queried. John hesitated and then explained that his father was never home.

He went on to describe how his father was distant and cold.

For the first time, John experienced feelings of hurt, disappointment, and anger toward his father. These new feelings were totally alien to John—he had never viewed his father in that light. But one of John's major issues was his difficulty in connecting with people; he always came across as distant and aloof. This behavior was having an effect on his sales career and all of his other relationships. His coworkers and friends described him as distant and cold.

As John released the powerful feelings he was holding about his father, life began to change for the better. John started to become more open and relaxed around people. This had an immediate effect on his sales and dramatically improved his relationships.

Human beings have a very difficult time seeing their parents in a negative light. It is our innate desire to hold our parents in high esteem regardless of how they made us feel. But we must reach down to our true feelings to clear the negative energy we are holding inside. We do not have to judge or hate our parents in order to release this energy. The release is only about how we *feel*, and that cannot be judged. Feelings simply exist in each of us. They are not good or bad, right or wrong—they just exist.

ANGER RELEASE MEDITATION

Begin by sitting on the floor in a comfortable position. You may lean on a chair or sofa for support. Do not lie down or you will go into sleep mode and lose your focus. Start to inhale and exhale on a count of three. This will help you take in additional oxygen and become more relaxed. Repeat this process ten to twelve times.

Now focus on one of your parents. Some people like to hold a photo to evoke memories and feelings. Try to remember how that parent made you feel as a child. Stay focused on how he or she made you *feel*. Do not concern yourself with their words or actions.

As you go deeper into your feelings, powerful emotions will

begin to emerge. Your success will depend upon your level of resistance and repression. It may take multiple meditations to stir up these deep-seated feelings. Once the feelings begin to surface, allow yourself to release them. This can be accomplished by crying or by feeling intense emotions. Anger may be your first reaction, but it is more of a surface emotion. The true block is deeper than anger, which is stimulated by other emotions. Go deeper and identify the true emotion. The anger may lead you to a feeling of unworthiness or shame. This is the true emotion you want to clear.

There are many layers to these deep chakra blocks. Do not expect to release a lifetime of pain in one sitting. This will become a process of release that will serve you well for the rest of your life. The more you release, the better you will feel. Each release will require a readjustment period based on the level of intensity. I have had several deep releases that left me with flu-like symptoms. You may experience body aches, headaches, and other uncomfortable feelings. When you expel negative energy, you are changing your body at its core. It will take some time for your body to catch up with your new vibration of energy. Be patient and do not attempt to rush the process. This is an organic process, not a linear one.

One of the greatest benefits of this kind of release is the effect it has on your physical body. You will feel physically lighter as the negative energy dissipates. Many people I speak with tell me how heavy they always feel. This sensation of body density is the result of repressed negative energy. With each release your energy becomes more flowing, resulting in a much lighter physical sensation.

When I am asked to describe this kind of release, I compare it to an exorcism. You can feel the negative energy leaving your body. This is an amazing sensation that will move you to a much higher spiritual level. Remain true to your feelings and you will see incredible results.

THE POWER OF YOUR MIND

Your mind works at both a conscious and an unconscious level. The conscious mind functions only when you are awake. This is the thinking section of your mind. Your ability to think, judge, reason, and choose is controlled in this part of your mind. The unconscious mind is the keeper of all memories, beliefs, patterns, and emotions. This section of the mind is working 24/7 and never takes a holiday or vacation. It is easy to see why the unconscious mind is the key to your success. The unconscious is also connected to your deepest emotions and to your chakras.

People continue destructive patterns of behavior because they are attacking their problems with their conscious mind. The belief is that a conscious action will solve the problem. This attitude has been at the heart of great distress for many people. It is extremely difficult for human beings to accept the fact that a conscious choice is not the answer.

There are numerous examples of this disconnection at work, but none is more compelling than the desire to lose weight. In 2022 people in the United States spent approximately $58 billion on weight-loss-related products and services. Americans purchased gym memberships, in-home exercise machines, weight loss programs, videos, and supplements, to name a few. A substantial amount of data about obesity is available from the Department of Health, the Food and Drug Administration, and many other agencies. The overall results indicate that over 40% of the US population is considered obese with an additional 30% considered to be overweight.

The conundrum is that we are spending a lot of money trying to lose weight but, in the end, achieving very different results. If conscious action were the true path to success, all the individuals who purchased these programs or machines would be very fit. The results tell us a very different story.

LATE-NIGHT TELEVISION

One night Gale wakes up at 3:00 A.M., unable to sleep. She is thirty-five pounds overweight and has been trying to shed pounds since she was a teenager. As she makes her way to the living room, there is a sudden rumble in her stomach. It's time for a late-night snack of delicious chocolate donuts and a glass of milk. She locates the remote and the blue pulsing light from the TV screen fills the dark room.

As Gale flips though the channels, she is bombarded by one weight-loss infomercial after another. Feeling depressed about her current physical situation, Gale is drawn to the latest gut-busting machine.

It looks so easy, and the results are amazing. Gale visualizes herself coming home every night and melting the inches away as she watches her favorite shows. At that moment she makes a conscious decision to purchase this latest miracle in weight-loss technology. There are several action steps that must take place to complete the transaction. Gale must find her credit card, write down the number, and dial the phone.

The next morning, she wakes up feeling great, knowing that she has taken action to solve her problem. Unfortunately, it will take four to six weeks for this invention to arrive at her home. This is a very stressful time for Gale at work, and by the time the machine arrives she has gained four additional pounds.

One day a deliveryman comes to her door with this incredible piece of equipment. Gale has a vague recollection of the night she ordered the machine and decides to set it up right in front of the television. The next day she decides to give this new miracle apparatus a spin. Within the first thirty seconds she realizes this type of machine is not right for her. To preserve some value, Gale converts it into a valet and promptly begins to hang her clothes there. This is the story of millions of people who shell out cold, hard cash for a weight-loss solution, only to see it rendered useless for the intended purpose.

The obvious question is why did Gale spend the money to deal with her weight issue and then fail miserably in the end? This has nothing to do with her desire to lose weight. On a conscious level she really wants to lose weight. Her issue is connected to an unconscious feeling or belief that she cannot lose weight. It is also possible that she is afraid to lose weight. If Gale were to lose forty pounds, her life would be dramatically different. She would start to receive more attention from men and maybe become more popular. This would bring up feelings that would make her uncomfortable. People like to keep things as they are, regardless of how bad the circumstance.

Never underestimate a person's desire to stay in his or her comfort zone. Change is something that most people want to avoid at all costs. The important issue is seeing your truth. When this happens, you will be able to release your negative feelings and clear the block that is holding you back.

NEW RULES

It took me some time to embrace these concepts. One of the most powerful revelations I have had is the understanding that my conscious choices do not mean as much as my belief system. Every day, people say they are going to lose weight, start a business, find a new job, or meet someone special. When you see these same people two years later, they are doing the same thing. The amazing thing is they are still telling you what they are going to do.

These are the members of the largest organization in the world, the justifiers' club. This is another example of people living in their conscious minds and not understanding why they never move forward. They also attract other justifiers to perpetuate their own belief system. Moving forward, you will realize how many of your conscious decisions do not deliver the results you desire. The key to success in this area is paying close attention to your results because they are telling you the truth. If you make a conscious decision to start a business and you fail to succeed, examine that result. This ultimate outcome is telling you how you really feel about yourself at a deep, unconscious level.

The ability to accept these results as your truth can prove to be quite challenging. Many people, like me in the old days, go into heavy denial and justification for a perceived failure. I would look for an excuse because that is what I was conditioned to do. Remember, this has nothing to do with assessing blame. You are not being judged or determining who is right or wrong. The important issue is seeing your truth. When this happens, you will be able to release your negative feelings and clear the block that is holding you back.

There are three fundamental rules to remember:

1. Your conscious decisions only have meaning when they are congruent with your unconscious beliefs and feelings.
2. Your results tell you the truth about how you really feel at a deep, unconscious level.
3. Denying this truth places you in a victim mentality that will hold you in your current position.

Remember these three simple rules and you will see dramatic changes in your life. There will be situations where you will struggle to understand how a certain result transpired. Your conscious mind will point to logic in an attempt to make sense of the outcome. Trying to make sense of the ultimate result is not the issue. You are seeking the truth, which the outcome is explaining in painful detail. You must accept your truth to move to the next level in business and in your life.

YOUR MAP IS COMPLETE BY AGE NINE

Earlier I discussed how the chakras are completely developed by the age of nine. The brain also develops and grows during the same time period. Up to 90 percent of your brain was developed, based on mass, by the time you were three years old. This ties into the first three chakras—base, sacral, and solar plexus—which develop in the same time period.

Most of your beliefs and patterns are developed by the age of three. During this time, you are absorbing a tremendous amount of energy and information.

You can see why people always say children are sponges. When a problem arises later in life, we believe it started at that time. The fact is that it started when you were a child. You simply may not have noticed it, or you may have been able to repress those feelings until it became too difficult to control.

Once again, logic tells us we should have noticed it earlier. But this has nothing to do with logic and everything to do with feelings. All core issues originated between conception and eight years of age.

When they become apparent is of little consequence.

7

DEALING WITH UNCONSCIOUS GUILT, SHAME AND FEAR

Unconscious feelings of guilt, shame and fear are the main emotions blocking success. Every great accomplishment is the result of someone overcoming deep-seated guilt, shame and fear. When you examine the most prolific achievements in human history, virtually all are prompted by an unshakable belief in a single idea. Successful people have the ability to overcome their own fears and the fears of others. When everyone says, "You are out of your mind," truly successful people dig in and push forward.

Each giant leap mankind has taken is the result of someone challenging conventional beliefs and fears. This fact can be traced through history. For example, people believed the world was flat because that was all they could see, and the alternative was terrifying.

Overcoming fear is deeply connected to your ability to believe in something most people cannot see.

Commitment to your belief is of critical importance, second only to your ability to remain patient. We live in a disposable society. If it doesn't work immediately, we move on to the next project.

You may be familiar with the Dyson upright vacuum cleaner. It is a snazzy yellow number with a very stylish design. The inventor, James Dyson, believed he could invent a vacuum cleaner with better suction that did not require the traditional bag to collect dirt. Over a five-year period, Dyson created 5,127 prototypes. When you break the numbers down it equals more than eighty-five prototypes per month.

In 1993 Dyson was ready to shop his new invention to the industry. To his dismay, Dyson found there was virtually no interest in his revolutionary new vacuum. Undeterred, he proceeded to market and sold the product himself. In 2005 Dyson's sales reached $10 billion worldwide.

In many cases it is easy to quit and hard to believe. Your ability to hold on to your dream in the face of adversity will serve you well. I am sure the Wright brothers faced tremendous skepticism when they attempted their memorable flight in 1903. The two former bicycle repair mechanics pushed their plane off a cliff in Kitty Hawk, North Carolina, and the rest is history. I wonder how many of the local residents agreed with their idea at the time. Once again, this is the story of belief in the face of adversity.

There is only one thing separating the millionaire from the average worker—courage! The ability to face fear is the key to unlimited success. Your greatest challenge is escaping your personally created *box of fear*. You must remember that fear is a conditioned belief. You were not born with fear—you learned how to be afraid.

I created the "box of fear" as a visual reference (see Figure 7.1). We have much higher retention when there is a visual image attached to a concept. This image is designed to help you frame the fears that you have been conditioned to believe are real. All fear is driven by a projected belief in an imagined outcome. If something has not yet happened, fear is merely a projection of the mind. These projections are the product of your conditioned beliefs and experiences.

Origin	Perpetuation
Your home	Your family, friends, school, religion, government, corporations, the media

FIGURE 7.1 Box of Fear

The box of fear has two key components:
1. *The origin.* This is the place you learned to be afraid. In most cases the fear started at home.
2. *Perpetuation.* Fear is perpetuated every day of your life by a number of outside sources.

You are always absorbing energy vibrations from your surroundings. As a baby, you have limited exposure to the outside world and nothing to compare your situation against. The only reality you know is based on the people and environment at home. Therefore, the majority of your belief system, which develops by the age of three, is based on your home life. The home you grew up in becomes your model for the future.

The level of fear in your home translates into a belief system that is passed on to the children. If your parents were always arguing about money, you may have established a negative association to it. You may be attaching money to problems or discord. If the belief in your home was that you must struggle to survive, this is the energy absorbed by the people in the household.

As you grow up and become more independent, you are exposed to more of the outside world. This helps give you a new perspective on the beliefs you absorbed as a child. However, in many cases the outside world simply perpetuates your internal fears.

KEY PERPETUATORS OF FEAR
Your Family
The fears you are carrying developed in your home. For this reason, it is easy to understand how your family would perpetuate those fears. They are carrying the same energy that created the fears in your unconscious mind. Every exposure to members of your family is a reminder of the fear you are trying to release.

Your Friends
Take a very close look at the people you are attracted to in the outside world. Do these people carry the same fears you see in yourself? I am sure you have noticed that successful people gravitate to one another. The same can be said for complainers and people who blame the world for their problems.

School
The classic American school system is traditionally a very scary place for people with an open mind. If you question the mechanics or procedures in practice, you will immediately be labeled a troublemaker. In school the teachers want everyone to fall in line and follow the rules. I do not mean to suggest we should not have any rules, especially in school. It would be nice if new ideas and questions were openly accepted.

I attended a rigid Catholic school in New York and have yet to recover. That might be a good title for my next book. We were disciplined with an iron hand by ruler-wielding nuns. If we got out of line, these gladiatorial nuns would be quick to slam a ruler across our knuckles with deadly accuracy.

I realize this did not happen to everyone, but many of us experienced school as a place of fear and guilt—fear of not doing well or of getting in trouble, and guilt if we did not live up to our parents' expectations.

In many ways, school sets people up for failure. We must

conform to a set of rules or be punished accordingly. This is a very linear system that teaches people to do everything in sequential steps. The system pushes us through a series of levels and then into a job so we can pay taxes for the rest of our lives. If you want to go out of sequence or challenge the regime in power, you will be dealt with accordingly.

Religion

This is an area I feel is very important to discuss. I am not here to praise or denounce anyone's religious beliefs. Each person experiences religion in their own way. But how the religious experience was transferred to you is a huge factor in your life.

Was it positioned as an entity of love or fear? Were you made to fear God if you did something wrong, for he would deal out harsh punishment? Or was God described as a loving being who forgives you and is always a positive force in your life?

Many people equate spirituality with religion. However, a person can be spiritual and not religious. Conversely, a person can be religious and not spiritual.

Spirituality is a universal concept based on love. In the world of spirituality there is no punishment, no sins or hell. Anything that is not pure love does not exist. In a world of pure love there can be no duality. You are pure love, or you are nothing.

Religion was created by man. All the guilt and fear that exists in religion has nothing to do with the true spirit of God. Religion also creates separation as people believe their religion is right while another person's is wrong.

Spirituality teaches us that we are all one energy and therefore all connected. Anything that causes us to feel separate is a function of the ego's desire to control and create discord.

Think about your life today and examine the influence religion has played in your belief system. Many of your current values and ideals are based on the religious experiences you had as a child.

Government

A government is designed to control people. The best way to control a population is by instilling fear in people. If they are afraid, they are less likely to act. This is a double-edged sword. On the one hand, we want people to know there are consequences for destructive actions such as murder and robbery; on the other hand, it is important to challenge conventional beliefs to keep a balance and encourage progress.

We have created scary organizations that can provoke fear by the mere mention of their initials. The CIA, FBI, and IRS are examples of such groups. We must maintain our ability to challenge convention to move away from a fearful existence.

Corporations

Major corporations have become as powerful as the government, and in some cases even more powerful. They have incredible assets and resources at their disposal. Many of their employees live in fear of losing their jobs because if that happens, they will lose their most valuable asset—benefits. Yes, people are so conditioned to fear the loss of benefits that they will stay in jobs they hate.

If you do not follow the rules (sounds a lot like school to me), you will be fired. Then you will lose your benefits and have to grovel to find another job. These fears are based on deep-seated beliefs that you first acquired at home.

The Media

I grew up in New York, the media capital of the world. We have more news and information coming at us than anywhere else. If you watch the news in the morning here you will find out about twenty-eight different ways you may be killed today. Most of the media is negative or sensationalized.

You must understand, these news organizations are in the business of making money. They are vying for ratings, which allow them to sell more advertising at a higher rate. This is more about economics than news. We are being fed the news that we crave as a fear-based society. The networks are airing what sells, and bad news sells. If there were a good news station, it would have no ratings and no revenue. The more negative media you absorb, the more negative your attitude and energy will be.

Coworkers

Like friends, your coworkers reflect exactly how you feel. Who do you hang around with at work? You may notice that the top producers hang out together or with no one at all. They realize that most of the people in the company are negative.

I remember seeing the same complaint sessions taking place at the same time every day in the break area. This group of people sat around spewing venom about the company and their managers. Who are you associating with at your office?

The list of fear-perpetuating influences can go on and on, but I am sure you get the point. The more you hang around fearful people and environments, the more fearful you become. You begin to absorb fear until it becomes woven into your DNA. It becomes part of your identity.

In sales and business, fear can be fatal. When you work from a position of fear, you are vibrating negative energy and attracting difficult situations and people. Pay attention to how many fearful thoughts you have each day.

Here are some fearful thoughts and tendencies that can slow you down:

- » Worrying about not making enough sales to pay your bills.
- » Focusing on just making enough to survive.
- » Judging people.
- » Feeling desperate.
- » Making poor decisions that are motivated by fear of loss.
- » Focusing on the budget and not the customer.

» Feeling you are lacking things in your life.

Think about the people you spend time with on a regular basis. If you are like most, you surround yourself with fear-based people who are struggling to survive. To become more successful, you would be well-served to get around those who are more productive and open to new ideas.

The people in your box of fear want to keep you as a member. As you begin to break away from that mindset, it is likely that you will become an outcast from that group. People who live in fear are not interested in those who choose to move on and make things happen. The box of fear can only be perpetuated by people who hold on to that kind of thinking and fearful energy. You must choose your place in this world. The only two choices are fear or love.

VICTIMS AND MASTERS

When you live in fear, you are functioning as a victim. The box of fear perpetuates the victim mentality. If you believe that life is happening to you, and you have no control over what is happening, you are in full victim mode.

Here are some victim issues to think about:

» When you lose a deal, do you immediately assess blame outside of yourself?
» Are you always making excuses for not accomplishing your goals?
» Do you feel you are not getting what you deserve?
» Do you believe you are not getting a fair deal?
» Are you constantly judging others?
» Do you always look for someone or something to blame

All these behaviors are directly connected to the victim mentality. When you look outside yourself for answers, you are giving up your power. The moment you allow an outside force to affect your success, you fall back into the victim mode. At that point you surrender your power and move back into the box of fear.

The first step in your transformation is ownership. Ownership is absolutely necessary if you want to become the master of your life and reach your true level of power. When something goes wrong, ask yourself, "Why did I create that situation and what is the lesson
I need to learn from it?"

As you become more adept at this process, you will notice a pattern developing. You may notice that you keep attracting the same type of client. If this is disturbing to you, it is time to search your feelings and look for a connection. This type of person repeatedly returns to your life to help you clear an emotional block that is holding you back.

Follow this process to help identify and clear your abundance blocks:

1. Be aware of how you feel when something goes wrong.
2. Examine the situation and determine whether it is part of a pattern.
3. Identify the feeling you have when the situation occurs.
4. Analyze your earlier life and find the origin of the feeling.
5. Release the negative feelings to clear the block.

The following story will help you put this information into context.

POOR BILLY

Billy was an entrepreneur and owner of a web design business. Billy was always attracting clients who did not pay on time and in some cases didn't pay at all. He was quick to offer credit and felt uncomfortable asking for his money. (Yes, it was *his* money because he did the work. It is important to realize that once you perform the service, it's your money.)

As a result of this behavior, he always felt like a victim. He was constantly complaining about how his difficult clients did not appreciate the work he did. Eventually his company dissolved because he was unable to sustain the cash flow necessary to stay in business.

I began to work with Billy on his victim feelings and we traced them back to his father. Billy's father had always told him that he was not smart and that he would be lucky to get a good manual labor job. He also made Billy feel he did not deserve much in life and should be happy with whatever he received.

Once we identified those origins, Billy was able to clear the anger he was holding toward his father. As the anger was released, he no longer had the compulsion to feel the feeling of *unworthiness*.

Billy had been attracting clients who reminded him of his father. As a result, he continually felt unworthy. Billy repeatedly created the same situation and the same feelings. His energy continued to create circumstances that eventually forced him to confront and clear those negative emotions.

Once the anger attached to the feeling of unworthiness was expelled, Billy no longer had the desire to feel unworthy. He was able to move forward and create a very successful business with great clients who always pay on time. You see, now he knows he is worthy of abundance.

THE GUILT FACTOR

The feeling of unconscious guilt is at the heart of many of our problems and issues. Guilt is the weapon of choice used by parents to control their children. As you can see, the ego's desire to control is extremely powerful. In most cases, parents are not using guilt on a conscious level. They have absorbed guilt energy for generations and passed it on to their children. Innately parents know they can use this guilt to manipulate and control their children.

Once the power of guilt is realized, it is then used in all areas of life. People begin to recognize the power of guilt in other situations.

It can be applied to relationships, employees, coworkers, friends, and family. The ability to manipulate effectively is tied directly to a person's level of skill in the use of guilt. This is an addictive power most people are not willing to give up. The ability to control others is the most addictive feeling on the planet. Beware of those who have mastered this skill, for they are truly dangerous.

The desire to control and manipulate is driven by fear. The ego believes it will be safe if it can control people and the environment.

This is why so-called *control freaks* are always micromanaging all aspects of work and the people involved with a project. There is an inherent fear that losing complete control of the situation will have disastrous results.

Parents teach children how to use guilt by using it on them so effectively. At a deep, unconscious level, children understand how to use guilt to get what they want in life. It only takes a few successful applications of the process to become hooked. The more fearful the person, the more he will have the desire to use guilt and manipulation.

I HAVE A PLAN

Jane is a single, thirty-four-year-old woman living in the city. She is well educated and has a successful career in the financial sector. Jane has her own apartment, an active social life, and is also dedicated to a rigorous fitness program. A look at this profile portrays a confident, self-assured woman on the rise.

Six months ago, Jane planned a ski trip with three friends. This was going to be a long overdue reunion of college roommates. Jane had been looking forward to this trip for months. All reservations had been made and nonrefundable deposits had been dispersed.

Two weeks before her scheduled trip her mother called to say that relatives were coming in from out of town. They would be arriving the day after Jane was leaving and would be gone before she returned. Jane explained the situation to her mother and expressed her disappointment in not being available to see her relatives. Without hesitation her mother asked if she could reschedule her trip to accommodate her relatives' visit.

Jane went into justification mode, explaining how the trip had been planned for months and that she would lose her deposit. Her mother was unwavering in her stand and wanted Jane to reconsider. "I am sure you can see them the next time they come, in five years," she said with sarcastic tone. As Jane hung up the phone her feelings of guilt began to bubble up. Her mother, a master manipulator, had placed a heavy dose of guilt on Jane. Would she go on the trip and defy her mother or capitulate and cancel the trip she was so looking forward to taking?

The feelings of guilt began to increase with each passing day. Another technique her mother used was the *freeze-out*. She did not call Jane after that initial call, to allow Jane's feelings of guilt to fester. Not knowing what her mother was thinking created more feelings of stress and guilt for Jane.

A few days before the trip, Jane called her friends to explain that she would not be able to come. Her mother had, once again, used her superior manipulative skills to achieve the desired result at the expense of her daughter.

The objective of manipulators is to win at all costs. They are only focused on the results and nothing else. The fact that Jane is unhappy is of no consequence to her mother. She achieved her objective and will be ready to use her process again when necessary.

SALES ORGANIZATION GUILT

These same guilt and manipulation techniques are used in the business world. A sales manager may use the exact same process to motivate his or her people.

Making salespeople feel they are not doing a good job can trigger similar feelings of guilt and shame. The intent is that they will start to feel bad and then have the desire to work harder. The effectiveness of this approach depends on the makeup of the individual. If similar techniques were used effectively by your parents they will transfer into the business world as well. You will be susceptible to the feelings of guilt you experienced as a child.

In the world of energy, we attract people who make us feel comfortable, and who activate familiar (even if unpleasant) feelings in us. You may notice that your boss triggers the same feelings that your mother or father did.

One of my clients was explaining how his boss was extremely critical of all his work. No matter what he did, the boss found something wrong with it. As my client examined these feelings, he realized his mother used to make him feel the same way.

Guilt, shame, and fear have long been viewed as the only way to motivate performance. Although the world has changed and some organizations are embracing more positive techniques, a large majority are still trapped in this model. It is important to realize how powerful these unconscious traits are and how difficult they are to break. The desire to manipulate through guilt has a long-standing place in history. It will take a major shift, which is currently in process, to eliminate this energy from the world.

There is a simple yet excellent way to monitor the feelings of guilt in your own life. Anytime you say you should or shouldn't do something, you are operating from a feeling of guilt. Paying attention to this will help you become more aware of the feelings that are truly motivating your actions. Another indicator is the need to justify your position. If you feel good about what you are doing, there is little need to justify it. When you find you are defending your position you are operating from a feeling of guilt and fear.

Here are some of my personal favorites:

» I should go visit my mother.
» I should be making more money.
» I should work harder and longer.
» I should have received the promotion.

» I should have been given my bonus.
» I shouldn't go out to play golf when there are things to do at home.
» I shouldn't eat that cake—I must lose weight.

Feelings of guilt will ultimately make you feel bad about yourself. When you say something like "I should be making more money," you are being critical of yourself. The underlying inference of the statement is that you are not doing well or not doing your best. When your feeling is focused on not doing well you begin to feel guilty and shameful. When you pay close attention to your true feelings, you will be amazed at how much guilt you are truly carrying.

As you release negative chakra energy, the feelings of guilt will go with it. You will no longer be driven by your unconscious guilt, shame, and fear. In addition, other people will no longer have the ability to manipulate you with these tactics. This can become very disturbing to parents who have been successfully using guilt as a controlling tool since the day you were born.

In the world of sales, your emotional drivers are integral to your vibration and attraction levels. It is critical to monitor how you feel at all times. This will be a recurring theme throughout this book. If you feel guilty about collecting money or closing a deal, it will surely impede your ability to thrive.

GUILT ABOUT RECEIVING MONEY
If you grew up in an environment of lack and fear, you may have trouble collecting your money. This was a major issue for me because I felt I didn't really deserve the money. Some people feel bad about asking for and collecting their hard-earned cash. Others have no such issue, as you well know from experience. But some people who are good collectors also feel fear or uncertainty about gathering the money owed to them.

In either case, negative feelings about receiving your money will affect your performance. There are only two feelings that rule the world: love and fear. All other feelings are based on these primary feelings. If you are feeling good about collecting your money, based on your internal joy, you are on the right track. When you perform a service or sell a product to someone and feel you have helped that person, you will feel joy. If you have a feeling of guilt or fear about the money you have just collected, you will feel bad.

When you are feeling bad or guilty it is important to understand why. In most cases, these feelings are the result of either a personal or an ethical issue. The personal issue stems from how you feel about yourself. It is a true barometer of your personal self-worth and confidence. In the case of ethics, it is connected to how you feel about what you are selling. If you feel that the product or service you are selling is lacking in value, it is natural to feel guilty about selling it. The obvious question is, why would you be selling something you do not believe in? The more obvious answer is, of course, that you are doing it for the money.

You will never become successful when guilt and fear are your emotional drivers. There may be temporary spikes in your income but ultimately the power of these negative feelings will catch up to you. When you are motivated by feelings of love and joy you will create success on a much higher level. As you help others you are simultaneously helping yourself. You experience a pure emotional high like no other.

8

HOW DO YOU FEEL?

On a crisp September morning in the early 1900s, a wealthy, distinguished gentleman in his late sixties strolled down a street in lower Manhattan. A mild wind swept across his face as he walked briskly, sporting a new black three-piece suit. In the distance, he saw three men working on a new building. As he moved closer, he could see that they were laying bricks.

He slowed his pace and watched as the three men methodically placed each brick in place. The gentleman stopped when he arrived at the location where the three men were working.

He posed the following question to each man: "Why are you doing this work?" The first man responded, "I'm doing it for the money." The second replied, "I'm doing it to take care of my family." The third man looked up slowly and pronounced, "I'm helping to build a cathedral."

The wealthy gentleman walked away with a twinkle in his eye, knowing that the third man would one day become a great success in business and in life. He was working on a much higher level than the others and understood the meaning behind the work he was doing. The feeling of meaning or purpose is what drives ordinary people to achieve extraordinary results.

A sale, like everything else in life, is about feelings. When you go out to sell something, you are motivated by your emotions. The higher the level of emotion you experience, the better you will be at selling a particular product or service. If you are emotionally disconnected and simply selling for the money, you will not be able to maintain the level of energy necessary to achieve true success. You must look at what you are doing as a mission. This is not about money, a promotion, or a new car. Focus on the mission of helping others and watch your income soar.

By now you realize that your success is directly related to how you feel. It does not matter if you work plenty of hours, make phone calls, go to seminars, and read every book on the market. In the end, these things are only useful if you feel the mission deep in your soul. This chapter will help you uncover your beliefs and tendencies. The more honest you are, the faster you will go.

Answer the following questions with the first thoughts that come to you. Go with your true feelings to get the most out of this exercise.

1. Why do you sell your product or service?
2. How much do you like what you sell? (Please rate from 1 to 10, where 10 means you love it and 1 means you hate it.)
3. How happy are you with your current income?
   A. Thrilled
   B. Very happy
   C. Somewhat happy
   D. Just okay
   E. Disappointed
4. Describe your financial history by finishing this statement: I have always . . .
   A. Made excellent money.
   B. Done well but would like to do better.
   C. Been inconsistent in my ability to earn money.
   D. Struggled financially.

5. What is the highest yearly income you believe you will earn in your life?

These questions are designed to help you gain a greater understanding of how you really feel about what you sell and about yourself. Let's review your answers.

Why do you sell your product or service? Did you always think of sales as a way to pay the bills and make money? Do you see what you sell as something that makes the world a better place? Are you passionate about what you are selling every day? Search your feelings and be honest with yourself. This is the map that connects you to your true feelings—to your soul.

How much do you like what you sell? Based on your answer to question 1, this should be pretty easy to understand. If you said you love it, make a list of the reasons. Then see how many of the reasons bring up a feeling of true joy. The more joy you feel, the better.

How happy are you with your current income? Many salespeople are simply making a living. They bounce from one sales job to another, looking for the right fit. Many salespeople struggle, not because of their skill level, but because of their passion level. If you are unable to generate excitement about the product you sell, it will be very difficult to consistently generate money. This is one of the main reasons so many salespeople experience extreme peaks and valleys in their incomes.

Your answer is also a reflection of how you value yourself. At this point, you are earning exactly what you believe you are worth. Most people say they should be making more money, but the universe always delivers based on your unconscious belief. You must accept that your income reflects your true feelings about your value. When your energy changes, so will your income.

Describe your financial history by finishing this statement: I have always... Your financial history is an important factor in your sales career and life. Most of your financial history is tied to what you learned about money as a child. If you believe you have to work very hard to just get by, that is the situation you will create for yourself. Your financial history is coded to your current energy and DNA. As you change your beliefs about money, your energy and code will be changed. Study your history and look for a pattern. This pattern is directly linked to your belief system. You will notice that the pattern is prevalent for yourself and for others in your family.

What is the highest yearly income you believe you will earn in your life? This is my favorite question, because if you are truly honest, your answer to this question tells the real story. In one of my classes a gentleman in his early fifties said he hoped he could earn $100,000 in one year. I asked why his greatest year ever was limited to that figure. He shrugged his shoulders and replied, "I have never been very good at making money."

Placing limitations on what you think you can earn stops the connection to your abundance gene. The best answer to this question is, "There is no limit to what I can earn." Believing in unlimited possibilities opens your flow of energy.

Your history has nothing to do with future earning potential. I have met dozens of people who struggled for years and suddenly had their financial life explode by connecting to the right situation and energy.

A few years ago, I met a man at a trade show in Philadelphia. He told me the story of his friend Bill, a struggling salesman, who had been fired from numerous jobs. Bill was living in a single room with his family when he went to a local electronics store and purchased a satellite dish. He went door to door until he sold the dish; then he took the profit and bought two dishes. Bill sold the two dishes and continued the process over and over again.

In the next seven years, Bill continued to build the business. He eventually sold his company for over $1 billion! There is no limit to what you can achieve in life. The only limits are those that you place on yourself. You must remove all limiting beliefs that hold you back.

Let this be your new mantra: *I have unlimited abundance and resources in all areas of my life.*

It is critical that you open your mind to unlimited possibilities in your life. The minute you place a cap on your income, you block your abundance. Never place limitations on yourself or use the past as a barometer. When you make the right energy shift, miracles will happen in your life.

GOOD VIBRATIONS

Every minute of every day, you are vibrating energy. This energy is related directly to the *law of attraction*. The law of attraction states that energy attracts similar energy, and you are always attracting things into your life. You attract people, opportunities, difficult situations, accidents . . . and anything else you can imagine.

Energy is working at all times based on your unconscious feelings and beliefs. There are two things happening with your flow of energy: You are always attracting, and you are always repelling. If you are feeling good, you are attracting positive things and repelling negative ones. The opposite is true when you are feeling bad. This is why we usually see a series of positive or negative events in our lives. The momentum of the energy you are feeling begins to attract more of the same feeling. This creates a cluster of energy which manifests as a sequence of events.

Once you accept the fact that you are attracting these things in your life, everything changes. You can no longer be a victim or claim you have bad luck. Your life is a reflection of the energy you are vibrating into the world. This energy attracts people and situations based on what you put out, without judgment. The energy does not make decisions or keep score. I often hear comments like, "I am a very good person yet I always have problems." But the energy of the universe does not distinguish whether you are good or bad, because it does not judge.

If you are vibrating negative, low energy, you are attracting the same thing. If you always worry about being overweight, you will attract conditions and situations to keep you overweight. If you always worry about money, you will never have enough. You get what you expect in this world.

The best way to make progress is simply to admit that you are in control. This is the first step in your journey to a higher level of enlightenment. Do not blame others, your parents, the economy, your education, or anything else for your current problems. Your life is a mirror of how you feel about yourself. Pay attention to your focus and watch success come right to your door.

In the world of sales your energy vibration is extremely important. You are attracting opportunities and clients based on the energy you exude. If you study your relationships with current clients, you can learn how you feel about yourself. If you have wonderful clients who are easy to deal with and pay on time, that reflects your attitude toward yourself. Conversely, if every client is a nightmare and causes all kinds of trouble, then that reflects how you feel.

Your clients and other people in your life are not there by mistake. These people did not appear randomly, as many people think. You brought these people into your life through your feelings and energy. Do not think for one second that they appeared for no reason.

Changing our thinking in this way is a huge step for most of us because it turns all responsibility over to us. Now there is no such thing as a bad break or unfortunate incident. Your entire life reflects how you really feel about yourself on all levels. You are now the *master of your life*.

Unfortunately, this is a job that most people would rather not have. It is much easier to be a victim and blame the world for your problems. I have been to countless sales meetings where people sat around the table and explained why they could not make a sale. Never focus on what you think you cannot do. Always focus your energy on positive results no matter what is going on around you. This will help you move through difficult situations very quickly.

Keep track of what you are attracting daily. It may be something as simple as a cup of coffee. Anytime you think of something, and it appears, you are attracting. Many of the things we receive seem to catch us by surprise, but these surprises are being generated by the more powerful *unconscious* feelings that we are not aware of. People may say something like, "Why would I *want* to lose my job?" Our results are based on unconscious feelings or energy. A deeper examination of your feelings will reveal the true feelings responsible for the result in question.

Another area to examine is the people around you who are the most difficult or annoying. In many cases these individuals are family members. The next time you see one of these people, walk up and say thank you. These are your best teachers, and they represent the most powerful lessons in your life. Remember, there are no mistakes or coincidences in this world. Everything happens based on your vibration of energy.

MANIFESTING 101

Spirituality has gone Hollywood to a large degree. Many people look at manifestation and spirituality as a mechanism to acquire material possessions. There is absolutely nothing wrong with wanting to attract the material possessions you desire. The universe wants every person on the planet to experience abundance and prosperity. The key here is understanding that true spirituality is about peace, harmony, and love. These are also some of the things we should be manifesting in our lives.

Manifesting means using the law of attraction with purpose. You are constantly manifesting things in your life. The problem is most people do not realize they attracted this person, opportunity, or incident to themselves. Something happens and we assume it is a coincidence or just good or bad luck. The reality is that we drew this person or situation based on our energy and focus at the time.

Try to remember a situation or time in your life when you *really* wanted something. It could have been anything—a pair of shoes, a new car, a job, or a favorite food. If you really wanted it and focused your energy, you were sure to receive it.

Years ago, I was looking for a new job. I focused on a certain income level and location. At the time, I was working on Long Island about thirty minutes from my home. One of my friends suggested I look in Manhattan, thinking I could make more money there.

I resisted because I did not want a long commute like so many of my friends had—many of them were traveling two hours each way. My thought was simply this: If I could secure a job near Penn Station for a certain amount of money, I would commute. Penn Station is the last stop on the train to Manhattan and only a forty-five-minute trip for me.

The interview process was moving along without much success. Then one day I received a call from an employment agency that I had contacted four years earlier. Since submitting my information four years earlier, I had not received a single call or contact of any kind. The woman from the agency told me about a great opportunity that was being offered in Manhattan. I interviewed and was offered the position. The salary was slightly higher than what I was targeting, and the office was directly across the street from Penn Station. This was a complete manifestation on all levels. It was the right salary, the right position, and the exact location I had placed in my mind.

As I said earlier, you are already manifesting. Now you can do it with purpose and direction. What you focus your energy on creates your reality in this world. Look at your life and compare it to what you are thinking about most of the time. I am sure that the internal picture will be very close to reality.

Successful manifestation requires three simple but powerful steps:

1. You must have a clear picture of what you desire and why you want it.

2. You must remove all mental barriers, limiting beliefs, doubt, and fear.
3. You must be vibrating a feeling of deserving and maintain your focus.

Let me break down these steps in more detail.

STEP 1

You must have a clear picture of what you desire and why you want it. The unconscious mind does not judge. It simply accepts what you enter as fact. Focus on what you want to create and forget about the money.

The next thing to do is look at your why? Why do you want to create it? Search your feelings and know why you want it. At a higher level of energy your why is connected to a feeling of love and service to others. If this is an ego-driven desire, it will not be as pure.

Feeling you truly deserve what you desire is another important factor. You may ask why do so many people with negative intentions create so much wealth and success. Remember, the unconscious mind does not judge. It simply responds to what it receives. It does not determine who is good or bad. This is not meant to condone such behavior. I am simply telling you how it happens.

If I asked you whether you deserved $10 million you would probably say yes. This is a conscious mind reaction to an obvious question. But the conscious mind, as you learned earlier, has little to do with whether you will receive $10 million. The unconscious mind rules your belief system and energy vibration. You will not manifest until you truly believe you deserve it at an unconscious level.

The next question is why do you want it? If you are manifesting a huge house in a fancy neighborhood, ask yourself, "What is driving my desire?" Your desires are triggered either by something you feel will bring joy or by your ego. When you are triggered by the ego, your manifestation is designed to prove a point. These are negative energy manifestations.

When you are driven by ego, the acquisition of possessions becomes a game. This is like a drug addict who needs more each time to achieve the same high. Joyful manifestations will have a much more powerful effect on your soul and on your long-term happiness. Be aware of the why because it is the key to happiness and peace.

STEP 2

You must remove all mental barriers, limiting beliefs, doubts, and fears. The best way to remove these obstacles is by bringing your fears and doubts to the surface. Many of us have been taught to repress what we fear, but repression has the opposite effect. When you repress a feeling, it eats you up inside. The only way to deal with repressed issues is to release the feeling. If you have doubts, fears, and limiting beliefs, you will block your manifestation.

I use a meditation technique to bring the underlying feelings to the surface. Imagine you have achieved the clear objective you outlined in step 1. For example, if your objective was to create an income of $500,000 per year in your business, imagine yourself in that situation. How will you feel when you have achieved that goal? Pay close attention to the feelings that come up when you are in that emotional state.

This technique can be extremely powerful when you allow yourself to truly reach the emotional state, feeling these conditions on all levels. The feelings that arise will tell you where you are blocked. One of my students, Danny, wanted his business to reach the $10 million level. When Danny entered this imagined state, he felt anxiety and shortness of breath. I asked him why having all of that success brought up such negative feelings. Danny said it was too much pressure and he did not think he was capable of managing the money. This fear was blocking his objective to turn his company into a $10 million business.

We all suffer from doubts in certain areas of life. If you have a clear but unrealized objective, there is something blocking your success. All of these blocks are rooted in a deep-seated fear. Expose the fear and remove the block. This may sound simple, but it is an extremely difficult emotional process. Knowing what the issue is will not be enough to remove it. You have to feel the emotion and then release the feeling. Use the chakra release process outlined in Chapter 6.

Practice this process on a regular basis and watch the world change. You can manifest whatever you want in this world. Remember, this works both ways—if you hold negative images and feelings, you will manifest those results. Be very aware of what you desire, for it is on its way to you—good or bad.

STEP 3

You must be vibrating joy and maintain your focus. People often say, "I will be happy when I attain a certain goal." To successfully manifest, you must be emotionally in the feeling or vibration of success before you can have it. Successful people see themselves in the position they are manifesting long before the actual day arrives. You have to vibrate the feeling of joy every day before you can achieve your ultimate goal. This is the true challenge with the manifestation process. Holding the dream and vibration long enough to see it through is essential.

Actors in Hollywood have been using this technique for years. Jim Carrey wrote himself a check for $10 million and carried it around with him. Many years later he signed a contract to appear in a film for $10 million. Is it that simple? Just write a check and carry it around with you for a few years.

Unfortunately, it is not that simple. One of the key elements is a willingness to do whatever it takes to succeed. You need a clear objective, commitment, and willingness to do what is necessary to make it happen. Your patience will be tested along the way as well. We all want things to happen when *we* think they should. That is your ego getting in the way. Focus on your objective and continue trusting that it will come—when you are ready to receive it.

Your dominant thoughts will play a major role in your ability to manifest. If you focus most of your thoughts on what you do not want, that is what you will receive. You must become the policeman of your own mind. Stay focused on your true, joyful desires, and miracles will occur.

Another major block is thinking too much about how it will happen. When you think about how you will achieve something, you are allowing the ego mind to enter. If this happens you begin to move into feelings of doubt and fear. "How can I ever raise the money to do this?" is one such thought. The how is not up to you. The universe decides how. Your job is to stay focused on what it is you truly desire.

ARE YOU A GOOD RECEIVER?

The Attractor Sales System™ is largely based on your ability to manifest and receive. To experience abundance, you must be able to receive from others. The inability to receive something for nothing will block your abundance. I always ask people at my seminars if they are good receivers. My first question is "How do you feel when you receive a compliment?" How you react to a compliment will tell you a lot about your ability to receive it. If you feel discomfort, on some level your ability to receive is not open.

I remember telling a friend I liked his shirt. He shrugged his shoulders and said, "This is an old shirt." He was unable to receive the energy of my compliment. His inability to receive also affected my energy, as I did not receive the joy of his acceptance of my compliment. When you do not receive, you create a double negative situation. Do not punish the person who is trying to help you feel better by not accepting the good vibes.

Most people are terrific givers and terrible receivers. You must become more selfish, in a good way, to experience abundance. Healthy selfishness is being self-interested. We have been conditioned to believe that by taking from others we are being bad people. This is a terrible burden to carry through life. You must place yourself in the first position in life. This is not selfish—it is the way the universe wants you to be.

Some people experience feelings of guilt when receiving something for nothing. We are conditioned to believe that we must do something in order to get something. That is not how it works in the attractor world. When you become an attractor, you will realize that you are able to bring the right people and situations into your life.

Attractors easily move into a flow state. The people who are struggling live in a world that believes forcing issues is the only way to get results. When you try to force something to happen, you meet resistance. As you begin to flow, life becomes easier, and business seems to find you.

Another block to receiving is keeping score. If you are always concerned with exactly what each person is giving you in return, you are in a negative space. Your actions should always be guided by your own feelings. If you feel like helping someone, just do it. Do not be concerned with what they can do for you in the future. I have helped many people and countless others have helped me. My desire to help is not driven by what they can do for me. When you are open and giving, you are always in a receiving mode. It is not necessary to be repaid by the person for whom you did a favor.

Look at the wealthy people you know or have seen. Do you think they are good receivers? You bet! A major block here is the feeling of guilt. Search your true feelings about receiving. You may be very surprised at what you find.

TUNING IN YOUR RADAR

When I was a kid, back before the digital age, we had radios with dials. You had to keep on turning the dial until it was in a perfect position to get clear reception. If you were off by the slightest margin, there would be static. I remember turning the dial left and right for ten minutes to assure clear reception to hear my favorite songs.

Most people are walking around like that old radio, not getting clear reception. Messages are coming in but, because your reception is not crystal clear, they are not coming through to you. As your radar improves, you will see people and situations in a different light. There are no coincidences in your new world. You will be more tuned in to the messages and the people coming into your life.

One of my clients was always complaining about the fact that his customers never paid him on time. I asked him why he did business with people who were continuously behind on their payments. "That's the market," he would say. He believed that all customers were difficult and did not pay on time. His belief system was transformed into energy that attracted exactly what he put out.

If you believe that all customers are difficult and will not pay on time, that is what you attract. This has nothing to do with the market, the economy, or the interest rates. It's all about the energy you are sending out into the world. During that same time period, I saw clients who had no such problems and always collected their fees on time. Why were these so-called market conditions only affecting my first client?

Be very aware of what you attract on a daily basis. As you become more tuned in, you will see how your energy is affecting you every day. Notice what happens on a day when you feel very positive. Then watch what happens when you feel negative and send out negative energy. You will be amazed at how these feelings are directly linked to the type of day you are having.

We have all experienced days when everything went right. Conversely, we have all had days when everything went wrong. These good and bad days are based on how you were feeling at the time. The key to your success in this area is called *holding the vibration*. Whenever you experienced a very positive day, week, or month, you were holding a positive energy vibration. The opposite is true when things are not going well.

The problem most people have is their inability to hold the positive energy vibration on a consistent basis. You may feel great for a few days or even weeks, and then something happens to send you into a negative vibration. In many cases, these episodes are the result of an *emotional trigger*. These triggers are buried deep in the unconscious mind and are tied to your belief system.

Let's say you have always struggled in sales. You have always been in the middle of the pack and never really broken through to the next level. Suddenly you get hot and start making big money. At that moment you shift to a higher level of energy vibration. Your streak continues for a month—and then disaster strikes. One of your best clients cancels a huge order. At that moment, all of your past failures come flooding into your consciousness. This triggers fear, your normal state, and away you go into a negative vibration.

The key here is catching yourself before you go into a downward spiral of negativity. Once you become aware of these emotional triggers, it will be easier to avoid the plunge into darkness. Your triggers are based on your belief system and the messages you received as a child. If you were always told things are going to be difficult, you will struggle because that is what you believe.

The best defense against this is to be aware of how you feel at all times. Keep your radar tuned in and do not allow others to bring you down. If you are always vibrating positive energy, eventually you will repel negative people and situations. Be aware of how you feel at all times to make this process work for you.

I like to think of it as driving on the highway. If you are driving along at seventy miles an hour and suddenly come to a complete stop, it will take a lot of energy to reach seventy again. Conversely, if you are going seventy and slow down to forty, it will be much easier to get back to seventy. There are times when we must crash emotionally to clear a major issue. In these cases, it is important to understand it is only a temporary setback.

THE POWER OF ACCEPTANCE

The ability to accept how you feel and where you are at a given moment is extremely powerful. When you are struggling, especially in sales, the tendency is to push harder. Even when you feel like a failure, your training teaches you to put your head down and plow through difficult times. The problem with this philosophy is that it blocks your energy.

Any time you do not feel your feelings you create resistance. This is where the feeling of pressure begins. Think about how you feel about yourself when things are not going well. Do you feel like a failure? Do you feel like a loser? Do you feel that you have no value?

When you get down on yourself, what do you do with those feelings? Do you resist and say, "I am not a failure" or do you get depressed? You may dismiss the feeling and pump yourself up. Conventional wisdom and training tell us to remain positive at all times. I talked about the importance of holding a positive vibration in the previous section.

Are you confused now by what seems to be a contradiction? If you allow yourself to feel like a failure, are you vibrating negative energy? The answer is no, you are actually in a very high vibration of acceptance. You have accepted that you feel like a failure at that moment. That does not mean you will be one for the rest of your life. You are simply allowing yourself to be in truth.

When you feel bad and pretend to feel good, you are in denial. This is a form of resistance, and it causes internal conflict. A person who is conflicted usually internalizes feelings, which results in physical problems or addictions. Anytime you are not true to your feelings, your energy level drops. Anytime you deny a feeling, you give it more power. Unresolved feelings continue to recycle and resurface until they are resolved.

When people go to Alcoholics Anonymous, the first thing they say is, "Hello, my name is _____ and I am an alcoholic." It would not be possible to move forward without admitting that you have the problem. This may seem like a very simple thing to do but in reality, it is quite difficult.

Many people who are alcoholics will never admit that they have a problem. They say they have the situation under control, and they can stop at any time. The reality is that these people are in denial. Facing your major issues is scary and most people lack the courage to do it.

A big factor in this step is allowance. You have to allow yourself to feel these emotions without judgment. When you are in this state the energy of the universe will flow through you. All of the resistance, pressure, and pain are eliminated the second you come clean. It is an extremely liberating and freeing experience.

When you feel you should be doing better or be in a nicer house, you are not accepting how you feel. This relates to the feelings of guilt and shame discussed earlier. One of the most powerful feelings in the universe is acceptance. I was always feeling I "should" be somewhere else in my life. This feeling hampered my growth and ability to feel joy. Once I moved into a feeling of acceptance, my entire world opened.

You must accept that everything is perfect at all times. You are exactly where you are supposed to be right now in your life. The moment you feel acceptance, you will be ready to move on to your next adventure. If you resist, you stay exactly where you are and remain stuck. Acceptance allows you to derive joy from life in an entirely different way. The simplest things, like walking your dog or playing catch with your children, will become your most joyful experiences.

AVOID THE COMPLAINERS

Jim was one of the most successful salespeople I ever worked with, but he was disliked by many of his peers. Jim was a loner who was extremely focused on his mission. While other salespeople sat around sipping coffee and complaining, Jim was out doing his thing. He never allowed himself to get caught up in company politics or negativity. As a young salesman, I watched him carefully in an effort to learn as much as I could.

I would ask Jim questions about his process and keys to success whenever the opportunity presented itself. His philosophy was simple: "I avoid all negative people and complainers because they slow you down. Most of these people are content to make a living and complain about life," he explained.

It is very easy to get sucked into a negative crowd. These are the people who become friends and go out for drinks after work to continue their complaining sessions. Most great salespeople and entrepreneurs are lone rangers, to a degree. I am not suggesting you cannot make friends or be sociable with coworkers. Just be sure you do not join the wrong crowd.

People resented Jim because he was always the number one salesperson. He received all the attention, won the contests, and made the big bonuses. Many considered him aloof and thought he had a bad attitude. The bottom line was that he focused on being the best and staying positive. When you are successful at anything, there will always be people who will be jealous.

Ask yourself this very important question: Is it more important to be liked or successful? As we grow up, our desire is to be accepted by others. When you break out of the pack, you are moving away from the majority and into the minority. For many people, it is more important to be accepted by the mob. They are fearful that once they become successful, people will see them in a negative light. This is a real fear that stops people from moving to higher levels.

JUDGE AND JURY

Another great lesson I learned from Jim was never to handicap a potential client. "Treat every prospect like they are worth a billion dollars" was his motto. Judging people is a very dangerous game and also a very low level of energy vibration. Judgment is always negative because it deals with absolutes. *Good or bad, right, or wrong, positive or negative* are all examples of absolute judgment.

The second you begin to judge you change your energy. A prospect can feel the judgment on an unconscious level. You must approach every person with the same level of enthusiasm and a positive attitude.

Many years ago, I was asked to speak for an organization in Brooklyn. This was an entrepreneurial group of small business owners. The event took place on a Saturday morning and was more than an hour's drive from my home. When I arrived, there were only five people in the audience. I was expecting fifty or more based on what I had been told. My first feeling was that it would be a complete waste of time. Then I caught myself and remembered the words of Yankee great Joe DiMaggio: "There is always some kid who may be seeing me for the first or last time. I owe him my best."

I quickly cleared my head and shifted to a positive state. The presentation was great, and the small group really loved it. Two months later I signed an excellent client who was referred to me by one of the people in that audience. In addition, I received several paid speaking engagements because of that day.

You never really know who you may be speaking to at a given time. Although your situation may not initially seem like a good opportunity, you never know where it may lead. Do not focus your energy on the one person you think will never do business with you. Look at the bigger picture and understand that every opportunity to meet someone is a gift. You never know where that meeting will take you. Do not burn bridges or leave people with bad feelings.

You may have to cross back over those same bridges someday. They will not do you any good if they are burned down.

If you do not think you are judgmental, take this little test. Pay attention to how many times a day you pass judgment. Any time you think a negative thought about another person or situation, you are in judgment. When you say something is good or bad, you are in judgment. When you look at someone and have a comment, you are in judgment. Try this for a day, or even just an hour, and see how well you do. I think you will be amazed at how many times a day you judge.

Be extremely aware of this attitude before you see a prospect. Every time you walk in with a preconceived feeling, you are judging. Remember, every person you meet is potentially worth a billion dollars to your business. If you treat every person you meet like that, you will see dramatically different results.

Our society judges everything. We have entire industries for critics. There are people who judge movies, restaurants, plays, clothing, art, and so on. We have been conditioned to judge first and ask questions later. This has become a very bad habit for the members of our society. Monitor your feelings and you will be amazed about how often you judge others.

I will never forget a man named Max who came into the bar I was working at one evening in the mid-1980s. At that time, I was bartending at a restaurant/club in the Greenwich Village section of New York City. Max was a diminutive man in his fifties. He was a Russian immigrant who spoke with a heavy accent.

Max sat down and ordered a scotch, straight up (no ice). He proceeded to order nine more and promptly slugged each one down. In less than an hour, he was stumbling around the bar. We all judged him as a degenerate lush. In the next month, he would come in a few times a week and follow the same script. All of the regulars and employees, including myself, made fun of his behavior and treated him accordingly.

One night he went on a real bender and drank himself into a stupor. He staggered out of the bar in worse shape than usual. Max was so drunk he barely made it to the street, where he fell to the ground. The restaurant had a huge floor-to-ceiling window in the front. I could see the entire street from my position behind the bar. As I saw him fall, I realized this was no ordinary evening.

I ran out to the street and dragged him back into the bar. One of the waitresses gave him some coffee and a few of us tried to help him sober up. As he became more lucid Max began to tell us his story. He had recently come here to start a new life for his family. His plan was to get established and then bring his wife to America. Six months after he arrived in America his wife died alone in Russia. He carried a tremendous burden of guilt and shame regarding this incident.

The entire group hearing this story felt a collective sadness. We were also ashamed of our judgment and harsh treatment of this poor little man. This was an invaluable lesson for all of us. Max became a regular and eventually stopped drinking alcohol of any kind. He released his sadness and was finally able to start his new life in America.

In most cases, we judge people and situations based on face value and nothing else. You never know what someone is carrying inside. Your ability to connect with others will be greatly enhanced when you stop judging.

THE MESSAGE FROM MANAGEMENT

It has often been said that the energy of an organization comes from the top and trickles down. This is evident in all facets of business and life. Each company reflects the leadership driving it. This is especially evident with coaches in sports. Teams pay for coaches they feel will bring a winning attitude. The team's attitude is based on the feeling the coach conveys to the players.

This attitude is not solely dependent on the coach's level of skill or expertise. All great leaders have the ability to inspire others to a higher level of achievement. Having technical skills is important, but without the ability to inspire, that skill is wasted. As a salesperson, manager, or entrepreneur, you have a responsibility to every person you touch. Your job is to make the people around you feel better.

As a salesperson, you may ask, "Why should I care if the people around me improve? It does not benefit me in any way." Every time you help someone you are moving yourself to a higher level. This is called an *extension of power,* and it draws positive energy to you, thus increasing your vibration. As you build more positive energy, you will attract better opportunities and advance your own career.

The extension of power is extremely important for managers and entrepreneurs. Your success is based on the production of others. Having the ability to extend your power will help your team do much better in all areas. This will create a feeling of camaraderie within the organization. Teams that win play as a unit and are willing to sacrifice for the overall good of the group. Do you want a band of mercenaries or a team that is watching out for each other?

Do not underestimate the power or the message of leadership.

The importance of leadership is evident in every aspect of the organization. It is critical that you send a positive message regardless of your position. Become a magnet for success and avoid your ego's temptation at all costs.

Your daily goal is to make every person you encounter feel better. Imagine how attractive you will be when you are generating that type of feeling. People gravitate to those who make them feel better about themselves. This is a noble goal that will translate into great success in all areas of your life.

NEGATIVE EGO IS YOUR ENEMY

It has been said that all successful people have big egos. Everyone has an ego. Ego and identity are required to have this human experience. The key to success, at a higher level, is knowing the difference between the ego and the negative ego.

Your negative ego is at the heart of most, if not all, of your problems. Think about how your ego is the catalyst of much of the trouble in your life. Judgment is all about ego. Envy, jealousy, guilt, shame, and anger are all driven by the ego's desire to control, judge, or be accepted. There is no place for the ego in business. It will always get in the way and force bad decisions.

Here is an easy way to determine how much your negative ego is involved in your daily life. Every time you make a decision, ask yourself this simple question: *Why?* What is motivating your decision at the moment? Are you acting on a positive feeling or is it an ego-driven decision? Do you want to prove a point, be right, or make a statement?

This is an easy way to monitor the influence of your negative ego.

When you make decisions based on what you feel is best for all involved, you are functioning at a high level. Take the ego out of the game and make your life easier. You have nothing to prove to anyone. Be happy with yourself and everything else will fall into place.

Ego Check Exam

On a scale of 0 to 100 percent, with 100 percent meaning all of the time, write the appropriate percentage next to each question. For example, if you feel you have to be right most of the time, your answer to the first question might be 75 percent.

1. How often do you feel you have to be right?
2. How often do you feel others are wrong?
3. How often do you feel someone is challenging your decision?
4. How often do you feel people are taking advantage of you?
5. How often do you feel you have to win, no matter what?
6. How often do you judge others?
7. How often are you jealous of others?
8. How often do you feel you are being cheated?
9. How often do you feel you do not receive what you deserved?
10. How often do you speak negatively about others?

> *Red flags:* Your ego is most powerful in any of the situations where you answered 50 percent or more. These are indications that you are being overtaken by your ego in these situations.

Here is what to look for in each area.

1. YOU HAVE TO BE RIGHT.

If you feel you have to be right all of the time, you are battling deep insecurity. This is linked to incidents and feelings you had as a child. You are trying to overcompensate by always being right. This is a fear-based desire. If you are not right, you may feel you are not smart enough or lack the competence to succeed.

2. OTHERS ARE ALWAYS WRONG.

This is also related to the insecurity you are carrying. Disregarding the feelings and opinions of others may also be a mirror of how you were treated as a child. If someone else is right, then you must have no value.

3. PEOPLE ARE CHALLENGING YOUR DECISIONS.

If people are constantly challenging your decisions, you are probably not confident enough in your ability. The energy you are sending out is prompting this reaction from others. Pay close attention to how you feel as you make decisions and check your level of conviction. In this situation, people tend to feel very defensive.

4. PEOPLE ARE ALWAYS TAKING ADVANTAGE OF YOU.

In this case, you have been trained to be a victim. You expect to do everything and receive little in return. Victims will constantly attract people to take advantage of them to perpetuate their own beliefs. This will give them the ability to complain and tell the world how right they are about everything.

5. YOU HAVE TO WIN.

Simply ask yourself why it is so important that you win every time. What does the perception of winning mean to you and how deeply is it tied to your identity? How do you feel if you lose? Do you feel guilty or inferior if you lose?

6. YOU FREQUENTLY JUDGE OTHERS.

Judgment is one of the most powerful energy blocks. When we judge others, we weaken our own energy. Society has conditioned us to judge everything about the outside world: how people look, what they wear, how they speak, and so on. Be aware of how often you judge others, and you will realize how negative this practice can be.

7. YOU OFTEN FEEL JEALOUS.

Do you always want what others have? Do you feel you should have things and others should not? If this pains you, then you have a deep feeling of inadequacy. You feel, on some level, that you are not valuable unless you have things or situations in your life comparable to what other people have.

8. YOU FEEL YOU ARE BEING CHEATED.

This is another sure sign that you see yourself as a victim and believe that the world is out to get you.

9. YOU FEEL YOU DON'T GET WHAT YOU DESERVE.

Remember, you always get what you deserve based on the energy you are vibrating on an unconscious level. Even though you may consciously feel you deserve better, your results indicate how you truly feel. Pay more attention to the results because they reflect your true feelings.

10. YOU SPEAK NEGATIVELY ABOUT OTHERS.

Does this really make you feel better? Search your true feelings for the answer to this one. This is a sure way to block positive energy in your life.

IMPOSING YOUR WILL

Many people believe the only way to succeed is by imposing their will on others. This is a true case of the negative ego running wild. People will argue that great leaders are strong-willed and very focused. However, having the will to succeed is not the same thing as imposing your will on others.

In most cases, the desire to impose your will is tied to the need to control, and the desire to totally control is connected to a deep-seated fear. The ego is blocking you from feeling your true feelings. The belief that you can impose your will on others is a true case of ego separation. In this situation, the ego believes that its superior will manipulate any situation or person to achieve a desired result.

When the desire is misused in this way, it uses force of will and disconnects you from your source of true power. This is a case of force versus flow. In the high-pressure world of sales, it is easy to move into this space. The pervading belief among salespeople and managers is that the only way to succeed is by forcing the issue. When you attempt to pressure prospects into buying, you are blocking your energy. In many cases this results in people repelling your offers or directions.

It is not necessary to impose your will to become successful. Anytime you have the desire to impose your will, search your feelings and see what is motivating you. The real issue may be linked to a feeling of insecurity, low self-esteem, or the belief that you have to prove your value. Try to determine the driver or motivator for this behavior.

A strong desire to impose your will is usually connected to deep insecurity. Your negative ego deals with this insecurity by trying to force a situation to suit itself. Bring up the real reason for your desire to control and release this feeling. You will be a much more productive person in the end. As I said earlier, the only way to do this is to *accept* the feeling and then let it go.

The true leader understands that force and fear will only work on a temporary basis. Eventually, using force will result in a revolt. Throughout history, whenever a vicious dictator tried to impose his will, he was eventually overthrown. It may have taken decades, but the result is inevitable. Instead of trying to control, use your will as a driving, positive force in your life.

BEING PRESENT

In today's society, too many people have lost their ability to be in the moment. You may be physically here, but you are thinking about being somewhere else. As you are speaking to me you are thinking about the call you have to make or the proposal you have to finish.

This is all connected to the world of distraction we have created. As I sit in a café on a busy street in Manhattan having coffee, I observe the waves of people walking down the street. It seems that every person is engaged in a cell phone conversation. These people seem to be oblivious to what is going on around them. It is amazing that more people are not struck by moving vehicles on these busy streets.

We are currently part of an epidemic caused by our inability to be quiet. We need constant outside stimulation throughout the day. This is an unhealthy way to live. Quiet time is imperative for a healthy mind. Quiet times provide the opportunity to connect to our souls and to a higher power.

When you are present in the moment, you are extremely powerful. Your focus and energy are directed to what is happening in front of you. There is no thought of the next call or the unfinished report. To become present at all times takes practice and commitment. You have to pay close attention to your thoughts to make sure you are not drifting.

Being present in the moment is extremely important in a sales environment where every detail counts. One moment of drifting can cost you dearly. If you miss an important point or detail, the deal could be lost.

I have a technique that will help you stay in the moment. Before you go to an appointment, meeting, or presentation, imagine you are climbing a mountain. See yourself hanging from the side of a cliff with your ropes, spikes, and hiking shoes. Understand the importance of every step as you continue to ascend. If you do not drive a spike in properly or if you forget to tie a knot, you could go crashing to your doom.

It is impossible to drift out of the moment when you are in an intense life-and-death situation. In such a case you must completely focus on what you have to do to deal with that particular situation.

Take this same approach with every appointment and client meeting. Using this simple visualization technique will place all of your attention on the business at hand.

If you are not focusing all of your energy on the current situation, you are cheating the people around you. This is unfair and disrespectful to others. How annoying is it when you are talking to someone, and they are taking calls on their cell phone or looking at a computer screen? Lock yourself into the task at hand.

THE PAST AND FUTURE

We spend our lives dragging up the past and projecting the future. However, this is a trap that must be avoided. The past is gone forever, and the future is yet to be. All you have is the current moment, so make the most of it. You can learn from the past and plan for the future, but that is all—you cannot live there. As you know, the best-laid plans are often derailed by an unexpected occurrence. In most cases, dwelling on what should or might have been will only drag you down.

How much time do you spend thinking about the past? Do you find yourself wondering what would have happened had you made different decisions? This is a dangerous trap that will lead to second-guessing and critical thoughts. It is easy to look back and imagine everything working out perfectly. Then you look at your own reality and begin to wonder about what might have been. The past is another place we go to conjure up guilt and shame. Feeling bad about an old decision or negative outcome is a sure way to open an old wound.

Projecting the future is equally damaging. Many people use their imaginations about the future to stop themselves from moving forward. This behavior is motivated by fear. People create imaginary obstacles to justify their fears. If they can project a negative result and then sell it to their friends and family, they can justify their lack of initiative.

Maryanne attended one of my "No More 9 to 5" seminars some time ago. This program teaches people how to start a business from home while keeping their day job. After the class, Maryanne purchased my home study course and participated in a number of tele classes. She seemed very excited about the prospect of starting her own business and gaining independence from her controlling family.

A few years later I received an e-mail from her. She asked me a few questions about getting started. I was surprised by the tone of this message, as she had been so excited about starting immediately. We exchanged a few e-mails and I suggested she give me a call. I asked her what she had been doing for the past few years. Maryanne became very defensive and told me about all the obstacles she had encountered while trying to get her business started. Her comments were all about what might happen if she moved forward. She made these statements:

> » I don't think I have enough money.
> » I am not sure I can sell this product.
> » The market doesn't seem to be right at this time.
> » I feel I need more information.
> » I was told I need a better business plan. (She was on her fourth.)

The future is a great place to project fear because no one can prove that you are wrong to be afraid. Since most people in the world are fearful, it is easy to find others to agree with you. If you find yourself using the future to halt your progress, you are in a fearful state. The sooner you admit it, the sooner you can move on to something new. Maryanne would never admit she was afraid to start the business. She is still looking for reasons not to get started, and I am sure she is finding plenty of them.

Learn your lessons well and do not repeat the same mistakes. Plan with the understanding that you must remain flexible and open to what life provides. Do not allow time to become your master. Live in the moment and make every minute count. Remain present and focused at all times. If you feel yourself drifting, stop and refocus on the moment. The moment you are living is all that really matters. Enjoy each moment and stop letting time run your life.

Being in the moment will have a dramatic impact on your ability as a salesperson. Your prospects will sense your elevated level of attention. This will create a different, more connected feeling for both you and the prospect. All of this will be happening on an unconscious level. The same thing happens in reverse when you are not in the moment. If you seem distracted, the prospect immediately feels the vacancy.

Make your client feel like he or she is the only person in the universe. That is what happens when you are fully focused on the moment. Everyone has the desire to feel special. Make your client feel comfortable and confident in your sincere intention to help, and you will see miraculous results.

DO YOU DESERVE IT?

How you feel about yourself will have a dramatic effect on your level of success. Your self-esteem is directly connected to your ability to thrive in the business environment. You may have the technical skill and personality to succeed, but without the right belief system, you are doomed. An essential belief to maintain is that you deserve the success you are working so hard to achieve. You must hold this belief at a deep, unconscious, emotional level. However, if it were that easy, everyone would lose weight and keep it off. As you know, most people do not lose weight and the nation's obesity level keeps going up. Conscious decisions have little to do with the result. Your success is linked to your belief system in your unconscious mind. If you really believe you can lose weight, you will.

Answer these questions:

» How much money should you be creating right now?
» How would you feel if you had $50 million? (Is there any guilt or fear?)
» What is your greatest fear?
» Do you believe you are more talented than your boss?
» Do you feel you are being treated fairly in business or at your job?

You must believe that you deserve abundance in your life. Any doubt or fear will stop you from moving forward and reaching your goals. It has nothing to do with what you are doing on a conscious level. It is all about how you see yourself on an unconscious level. Stay attuned to your feelings, and the emotions that are blocking you will surface.

Anytime you want to resist a feeling, that is the feeling you must allow to surface. Not allowing the feeling to surface is blocking you from getting what you want.

WHAT IS YOUR INTENTION?

When I was a sales manager and something went wrong, my first thought was, "What was the intention of the salesperson?" I was less concerned with the incident itself—the intention of the salesperson was far more important to me. Everyone makes mistakes, especially in the dynamic world of sales. But if someone was deliberately trying to deceive me or take advantage of the company, then the incident itself became an issue.

Years ago, I was managing fourteen advertising sales reps at a local newspaper. Each salesperson had the ability to negotiate gas barter with a local service station. The station would receive a quarter-page ad each week in exchange for a tank of gas. I would sign off on the barter on a weekly basis for the accounting department.

One of the reps needed repair work on her car and started to give the station a full-page ad each week in exchange for the repairs. This was not part of the barter and was not authorized by the company. She slipped the paperwork through for a few weeks in a sneaky manner, until I caught it. When I confronted the rep, she tried to backpedal and make an excuse.

The bottom line: Her intention was to deceive me and take advantage of the situation. She was terminated immediately and did not receive severance pay. In addition, she was responsible for the lost revenue from the gas station ads, which was deducted from her last paycheck.

Your intention in sales and in life is extremely important. Your integrity and your word are all that you have in this world. If your intentions are always pure, you will achieve extraordinary levels of success. Be sure to always focus on the client's best interest. Do not think about money, commissions, bonuses, or other external trappings. Focus your intention on helping another person on some level.

When you move to this higher level, you transcend the world of basic selling and move to the world of *spiritual selling*. In this state, you are functioning on a completely different level. Your clients and prospects will feel this and be drawn to your energy. At this point, you are no longer a salesperson. All the pressures and feelings attached to being a salesperson are dissolved. In this elevated state of peace, you will become much more effective in all areas of business and life.

Transcending the material world is the ultimate level of success in all areas of life. When you remove external motivators and work from within, you are in your true *space of power*. There you will find an extraordinary feeling of peace and tranquility. When you remove the ego's desire for external gain and work from a position of purity, you are unstoppable.

Move into your space of power and release your desire to be someone or something that you are not. Work from your gut and follow your instincts. You already know exactly what to do in this life. Do you have the courage to follow your feelings and fulfill your true destiny? I believe you have this ability and much more. Simply allow it to surface.

Believe in yourself no matter what the critics say. Your true power cannot be denied if you truly believe.

9

TAKING THE EASY ROAD

Every day we make decisions that impact our lives. Some of these choices are less dramatic and a bit mundane. What to wear, where to go for lunch, and which train we should catch are in that category. Other decisions carry much more weight and are linked directly to the level of happiness we will have in our lives. The biggest decisions we face revolve around choosing a partner and career. We will spend most of our lives with our partners and working. Poor choices in these two areas will dramatically affect your level of happiness.

The universe wants you to have a joyful and prosperous life. When you make the right choices, life is easy and flowing. Choices are made based on a person's level of internal trust. Your ability to trust your instincts is tied to your level of confidence. If you are constantly second-guessing yourself, you are not trusting your gut feelings.

Another sign of a low confidence level is the inability to make a decision. One of the most important qualities of a leader is the ability to make decisions and then stand behind them. If you are always in a fearful state, it is impossible to make good decisions. This creates a feeling of doubt that clouds your energy and impairs your ability to make the right decision.

There is actually no such thing as right and wrong in the universe because there are no absolutes. The "right" decision I am speaking of is the choice that is best for you. How you view your decision depends on your perception of each situation.

The trouble begins when you are made to feel that your gut instincts are incorrect. You may have told your mother about a person who made you feel uncomfortable. If your mother told you it was ridiculous to feel that way, your gut instinct was questioned. As children, we believe our parents' word is law. When your feelings are dismissed over a period of time, you begin to doubt your instincts. These gut feelings are the most valuable asset we have in this world. Your feelings are connected to the unlimited power of the universe. Every time you doubt your instincts, you are weakening your connection to the wisdom of the universe.

TONY THE MILLIONAIRE

In 1981 I met Tony at his very successful New York nightclub. I was there to apply for a job as a bartender. Fortunately, I was hired and started working a few days later. Over time, I had many opportunities to speak with Tony about business. He told me how, as a young man, he had started a shoe business and became a millionaire by the age of thirty-one. Then he explained how he lost it all in three years.

Tony had been in a number of different businesses over the years. He had made and lost more money than most people see in a lifetime. The most valuable lesson I learned from Tony was to trust my instincts. "Every time I lost everything it was when I went against my gut," he explained. He spoke of many people who gave him bad advice and others who took advantage of his inexperience.

In the end, Tony felt he was a smarter, more appreciative

entrepreneur because of his failures. He learned hard lessons that each of us must experience. The bottom line was he needed to realize that his true feelings were the gateway to success.

The correct road for you will be connected to your gut feelings. When you follow your truth, the right doors will open in your life. Every time you doubt yourself and resist your feelings, you are moving backward. Many of your decisions may be made due to feelings of guilt and fear. When this happens, you are making a decision to make someone else happy. In many cases, you do this at your own expense.

THE POWER OF TRUST

Becoming spiritual requires a strong level of trust. You believe in something you cannot see or prove by today's scientific standards. Your capacity to trust others and the universe begins with the ability to trust yourself. This skill—yes, it is a skill—is connected to your feeling of self-worth and sense of importance. You must see yourself and your individual contribution as meaningful to the world. When you place yourself in this elevated light, it is impossible to minimize your value as a human being.

Trusting your internal guidance system is the key to finding your true purpose on this planet. If you find yourself constantly changing your decisions or allowing others to move you away from your path, it is time for a change. Any time you capitulate to others, it is important to understand the feeling driving your decision. The choice not to follow your gut is based on a fear of the outcome. You may believe that following your feelings will make others unhappy. In this case, you are placing the feelings of others above your own. The universe does not want you to place yourself second or third or fourth.

The more you trust and follow your own feelings, the more powerful you will become. Each time you trust these feelings you are elevating your vibration of energy. As this happens, you begin to attract people and opportunities that are congruent with your true purpose. Doors will swing open and life will become much easier.

The most difficult part of this transition is the resistance you will receive from others. You will be seen as selfish or dogmatic. When you begin to meet this resistance, do not panic. This is a sign that you are now moving away from the old and closer to the new. The new in this case is your true purpose and desire.

Every decision you make from this point forward can be tested on the simple love versus fear scale I mentioned in Chapter 3. When you are feeling joyful about your decision, it is the right choice for you. Any time you feel a level of discomfort or fear, you are not following your gut. The key here is being true to how you really feel and not trying to justify decisions based on fearful thoughts.

ATTACHING EVERYTHING TO THE OUTCOME

The business of sales is a very easy game to play from the standpoint of dollars and cents. You either make the sale or you don't. There are no points for almost making the sale. From that perspective, this is a very black-and-white world. You enter an appointment with the outcome in mind: Your goal is to make the sale or die trying. If you are successful and close the deal, you are a hero. Should you fail to close, the encounter is considered a failure. I know there are other variables, but this is the basic scenario.

When you enter a sales opportunity with the outcome in mind, you are vibrating with fearful energy. The best salespeople on the planet never go in thinking about the outcome. They are focused on connecting with the prospect on a higher level. This is a much higher feeling of vibration, and the prospect will feel it, too.

When I started my speaking career, the only concern I had was to do a good job and deliver value to the audience. Then I started to add products that I would offer from the front of the room. In the speaking world, this is called selling from the platform or stage.

Being a big researcher, I went out to find any and all information I could on the topic of platform selling. I had some difficulty but was able to locate some useful information; today there is much more material available on the subject. All of these books and programs were filled with techniques on how to sell more from the front of the room. There were certain phrases you should use, a specific time to make the offer, and a pricing strategy. Another element outlined was the percentage of sales per person necessary to achieve success.

Having done all this research, the next time I spoke I was confident I could employ these strategies and make a fortune in product sales. I could imagine the entire audience running to the back of the room to gobble up my valuable information. However, while I did not realize it at the time, these thoughts were having an effect on how I felt when I was speaking. Instead of being focused on delivering a great presentation, I started to think about the sales I would make at the end of the talk. I was now focused on the outcome instead of on the task at hand.

As I failed to sell the percentage deemed necessary to be successful, I started to doubt my level of skill. This brought up my ingrained tendency to be critical of myself. I now realize this was all designed to make me feel worse about myself. It was set up, orchestrated by me to bring up feelings of failure I was trying to avoid. I had replaced the joy I always felt when speaking at an event with a grim tale of poor sales.

In the years that followed, before I learned about the chakra energy release work, I tried every technique known to man. Maybe it was the price, the offer, or the name of the product. I drove myself crazy looking for a logical answer. People seemed to like my presentation and relate to my material, so why wasn't anyone buying anything?

I now know that the reason for all these struggles was related to my focus at the time. Now I never think about how many sales I will make in the back of the room. My job is to connect to the audience and move them to a higher level of energy vibration. When you convey that type of energy, people feel the joy and want more of you. This has translated into more dollars and, more importantly, a lot more joy.

The next time you are preparing for a sales call or presentation, stop for a moment. Make sure you are not concerning yourself with the outcome. The only important issue is to connect with the people you are meeting. When you make a true connection, the sale takes care of itself.

STOP BUILDING NEW HIGHWAYS

One of our deeply ingrained societal beliefs is that everything worthwhile has to be very difficult. We are all on journeys designed to help us learn lessons. It has been said that no one ever learned anything from success. Most of the great lessons we learn in life are the result of failure and pain. If everything were easy there would be no reason to look inside and explore ourselves on a deeper level. I am all for earning my stripes and doing the work necessary to succeed, but it would be nice to earn those stripes while moving in the desired direction.

When the answer is not apparent, people feel compelled to take action and start building new highways. Their underlying theory is that any action is better than inaction. But in many cases taking action for action's sake is not the best idea. The belief that building a new highway is necessary to reach your ultimate goal is flawed. There is a simple path waiting to lead you to the perfect location.

Finding this simple path requires patience and faith. You may have to relax and wait for the right door to open or person to appear. In some cases, especially when you are a bit confused, you can ask the universe for some help. Any time I am unsure about my next step, I stop everything I am doing. This gives the situation some much-needed space to breathe. When I practice this simple philosophy, all answers come to me relatively quickly.

One of the techniques I like to employ in these situations is the "ask for guidance" meditation. All you have to do is sit quietly and ask the universe for help with a particular situation. You will always receive an answer.

A few years ago, I was at a crossroads with my business. I had the idea for *Spiritual Selling* and was also working on a few other concepts. One of the first steps in my process regarding a new book or program is securing the Internet domain name. I am partial to the *.com* name above all others as it remains the king of the online world. When I typed in "spiritual selling" to check whether the .com version was available, I was sad to see that it was taken. I attempted to contact the owner to buy the name, but I never received a response. Was this the universe telling me to move in a different direction?

I began my "ask for guidance" meditation. The request I posed was, "Please guide me in the direction that will give my life the most meaning and purpose." After going through this process, a number of times, I had faith in the universe and was patiently waiting for my answer. I also realized the magnitude of the question and accepted the fact it may take a while before I received my answer.

A few days later I received an e-mail from a man named Wade, with whom I had spoken more than a year earlier. This gentleman had listened in on one of my telephone seminars. At that time Wade had called me with some questions regarding his new business venture. We spoke a few times and he insisted on paying me for my time. I knew he was going through a rough patch, and I would not accept any money from him. He thanked me and was very appreciative.

Wade is very technically savvy and was working on some online business ideas. He was receiving my newsletters and knew I was launching a new program called *Spiritual Selling*. In his e-mail, Wade explained how he had been checking for domain names when he came upon *spiritualselling.com*. Knowing I would be interested in the name, he purchased it on my behalf.

My answer had come in the most profound way possible. If there was any doubt about my next step, it was erased that day. Six months later I secured the deal for this book. The messages of the universe are not always as overt as my spiritualselling.com story, but the answers are all waiting for you whenever you are ready to receive them.

It can be challenging to allow yourself to be guided because you are giving up control. The ego wants to believe it is controlling your destiny. All the ego does is keep you away from your true path. When you let go and allow the ultimate wisdom of the universe to guide you, life becomes easy. Living this way also relieves all the pressure to make the right decision. All you have to do is ask for guidance and the answers will come to you.

Once again, this will require faith and trust. You can continue to build new highways and expend a lot of energy trying to find the right direction. Either way, ultimately you will end up where you are meant to go. But it is much easier to follow the path that is waiting to help you.

The next time you feel compelled to start building, stop for a moment and ask for some help. You may be amazed at how much easier your life can be. There is a simple path filled with beautiful flowers and a flowing stream just waiting for you. I promise you, following this path will prove to be a much more interesting and fulfilling journey.

10

MAINTAINING YOUR ENERGY

Selling requires a lot of energy, so it is critical to maintain a consistent level of energy to be successful. Unlike other jobs, selling requires you to be always at your best. Many people who have office jobs can sleepwalk through the day. In sales, you do not have that luxury. Any time you are not functioning at 100 percent costs you money.

I view my business as a marathon and prepare for the long haul. Anyone can push hard for a few months to drive sales. In the big picture that is no great accomplishment. Maintaining your energy involves pacing and consistency. Many salespeople experience peaks and valleys because they are unable to maintain a consistent level of energy.

Stress is a big part of business and sales. You know your mind and body better than anyone else. When you begin to feel fatigued, it is time to take your foot off the gas pedal and rest. Knowing how and when to recharge your batteries is the key to long-term success. Scheduling your time is the best way to consistently assure success. This will help you remain on an even keel, avoiding the usual peaks and valleys of the sales world. You must be disciplined and stick to your schedule. One day off can recharge you for weeks. Not taking that day can have a negative impact on your energy for weeks.

MANAGING YOUR SCHEDULE

In sales, your calendar is a flowing and dynamic document. Managing your time in an efficient manner is critical to your success. Time is the most valuable asset in the sales game. I manage my schedule by placing my days into categories. This assures that I am consistent each month. It also helps me look ahead and plan based on what activity will be emphasized on a given day.

Action days are the most intense days on my calendar. These are the days that revolve around generating business. They consist of the activities necessary to produce revenue. Action day activities include:

> » Appointments.
> » Presentations.
> » Speaking at events.
> » Seeing existing clients.
> » Networking.

Marketing days revolve around building lead funnels (this is detailed in Chapter 16). On these days I will plan my marketing, make contacts, and build relationships. These days are more strategic in nature. Marketing is a key element to long-term sales success.

Marketing day activities include:

> » Making contacts.
> » Writing articles.
> » Sending newsletters.

» Looking for events.

» Connecting with potential marketing partners.

Preparation days are used to do homework and take care of paperwork and details. On these days I do not make calls or interact with clients. This is a true back-office day. Preparing for appointments is one of the keys to closing more deals. Do not underestimate the importance of preparation and organization.

Down days are days off. Anticipating when you will need a day off will do wonders for your long-term success. The key is to anticipate the need *before* you reach the point of no return. Do not wait until you are completely stressed and burned out to take a day off. Another key factor in this process is your definition of a day off.

The day off is most effective when you completely detach yourself from work. Do not look at e-mails, answer your cell phone, or call in for messages. One clear day with no thoughts of work is a true gift.

Know when you will need that day based on your schedule. This will serve you well in the long run and help you remain at a consistent energy level. To avoid a significant drop in energy, I book my down days in advance. As I approach the end of one month, I begin to look at the month ahead. Based on my commitments and activities, I select at least one day per month to take off. The key here is to adhere to your own rule. Once this day is blocked out, you do not schedule any appointments or calls for that date.

One of my favorite activities on a down day is going to a movie. This is a great place to sit back and not think too much. The down day is all about you being good to yourself. I guarantee these will become days you look forward to each month.

Figure 10.1 is a sample calendar that uses the following codes:

A = Action Day   **M** = Marketing Day
P = Preparation Day   **D** = Down Day

Sun	Mon	Tue	Wed	Thu	Fri	Sat
						1
2	3 A	4 A	5 P	6 A	7 M	8
9	10 A	11 P	12 A	13 A	14 M	15
16	17 A	18 P	19 A	20 M	21 D	22
23	24 A	25 A	26 M	27 P	28 M	29
30	31 A					

FIGURE 10.1 Sample Calendar

This sample is designed to give you a visual point of reference. As you can see, each day is assigned a function. This will help you remain consistent and focused. Some people like to assign specific functions to days of the week—for example, every Friday is marketing day. Work with your calendar until you develop a system that is comfortable for you.

You should have at least one down day per month, plus at least four weeks of vacation per year. I know this may sound extreme to some people, but remember: This is a marathon, and you must maintain a consistently high level of energy to succeed.

PHYSICAL FITNESS

You will maintain a much higher level of energy if you are physically fit. Many busy people do not make time for exercise, and they sacrifice their health for money. This is another short-term philosophy. When you are physically fit, you are more focused and productive. Energy is generated by your mind and body. The better you feel, the more energy you will have daily.

It is not necessary to follow an extreme regimen of exercise to stay in shape. A simple workout of thirty minutes every other day will do the job. This can be any type of activity. Choose the type of exercise that is best suited for you. Be sure to select something you like in order to assure consistency. It could be running, yoga, weight training, or boxing. Making time for exercise is key to your success.

Another factor is the time of day you exercise. Some people like the morning while others prefer lunchtime or evening. I am not a morning person, so I like to work out in the middle of the day. It gives me energy and breaks up the day. You know your body clock better than anyone else, so select the best time for you.

MENTAL CLARITY

Selling can be mentally draining. You must maintain your mental focus and clarity. Many of us get overloaded with work, which causes stress and leads to mistakes. Every mistake costs time and money. Remaining mentally strong will be a great asset to your career in sales.

In the next section, I share some of the best techniques I know to help you in this area. These concepts will help you maintain a much higher level of energy on a daily basis. In sales, anytime you are not 100 percent focused, it will cost you. The goal is to remain steady and always operate at maximum capacity.

JOE'S 11 TIPS TO STAY ENERGIZED

Tip 1: End the Day

Many people have their brains going 24/7 and never take a break. This causes exhaustion and fatigue. Your brain has to rest just as your body does. If you run ten miles, you would hydrate your body and rest. Similarly, when you go through a stressful period, rest your brain and recharge. Ending the day means that at a certain point, you shut down all thinking about work. This will help you relax and, in some cases, you will get a better night of sleep. Thinking about work before going to bed is not conducive to sleeping well.

Each day is different in business, which makes it virtually impossible to set the same daily ending time. You may work late one evening and end the day at 10 P.M. while another day allows you to stop at 3 P.M. Once you decide to end the day, apply the same rules as for the down day: no e-mails, phone calls, or thoughts of work from that point forward. Clear your mind and be sure to end each day.

Tip 2: Change Negative Focus

There are times when your mind is filled with negative thoughts. Many people try to push through these time periods by attempting to steamroll over their feelings. Instead of forcing the issue, change your focus. Take your mind off the issue by doing something else, like going to a movie, meeting friends for dinner, listening to music, and so on.

In many cases, people are determined to keep on pushing when things are not going well. This usually causes more stress and tension. When you feel pressured or tense, break your focus by doing something different. Release negativity as quickly as possible to avoid slumps.

Tip 3: Surround Yourself with Positive People

Positive people are energizing, and negative people are very draining. It is not difficult to find a group that is constantly complaining and seeing the half-empty glass. Make sure you surround yourself with people of like mind and spirit. The people around you are attracted to your vibration of energy. You may notice how different people are attracted to you at certain times. Monitor how you are feeling, and you will see that same feeling reflected in the people around you. If you are unhappy with the people surrounding, you it is time to shift your energy.

Tip 4: Lighten Up

Do not take life, or yourself, too seriously. Most of the time, the things we feel stressed about are not so important. A lot of stress in business revolves around self-importance. This is a strong ego trait of insecure people. If you feel every situation is life or death, you are sure to feel tension. We all want to do a great job but maintain our balance and humanity. You will live a lot longer.

Tip 5: Watch Less TV

Television can be very entertaining, filled with great information, or make you laugh. It can also be a mind-numbing device that zaps your creativity. A large portion of the programming available today is negative and depressing. Coming home from work, throwing yourself on the sofa, and clicking the remote has become the standard for too many people. This is a bad habit. The next time you find yourself mindlessly flipping through the channels looking for something to watch, stop and turn it off. I am sure you can find something more constructive to fill your time.

Tip 6: Avoid the News

I know you want to be up to date with world events, but most news is very depressing. When was the last time you turned on the evening news and felt uplifted? Bad news sells, and that is why we see so much of it. My suggestion is to avoid it as much as possible, especially at night before bed. The media can be a source of depression and give you a negative outlook on the future.

Tip 7: Listen to More Music

Listening to music is one of the best ways to stay in a positive state of mind. Instead of listening to the sounds of a droning television, turn up your favorite tunes. It is impossible to be in a bad mood when you are listening to your favorite music.

Tip 8: Stop Rushing

The act of rushing throughout the day provides a high for many people. That feeling of pressure can be very exciting and addictive. But rushing is a bad habit that serves no positive purpose. If you find you are always in a rush, ask yourself "Why am I acting this way?" For many, it is an ego-driven habit designed to make you feel important. Do not make excuses and say that you are always very busy. Take inventory and see if you are rushing for the sake of your ego.

This behavior is a choice people make to help mask deep insecurities. It also gives people a false sense of value, which stems from the belief that if I'm rushing, I must be doing something important. It is a false feeling designed to feed the ego and move you away from your true feelings.

Tip 9: Laugh More

Laughter has proven to be one of the best things you can do for your health. It boosts the immune system and helps your attitude. When you laugh, life becomes a lot more fun. Make laughter a priority in your life. Surround yourself with people who are joyful and full of life. It is very difficult to feel bad when you are laughing.

Tip 10: Meditate

Clearing your mind through meditation has extraordinary benefits. You do not have to meditate for hours at a time. Try this simple exercise a few times a day and see how you feel. It takes thirty seconds to a minute. I am sure you can spare that amount of time.

Sit quietly with your hands unclasped and your legs and feet uncrossed. Close your eyes and breathe in on the count of three. Then exhale through your nose on a three count. Repeat this process three or four times. You will be amazed at how relaxed you feel in such a short period of time.

Tip 11: Eat Less

As you move into higher energy your body will not require as much food. In addition, your desire for unhealthy food will be diminished. I have seen this happen in many of my clients over the years as they have elevated their energy levels.

When you feel heavy and bloated you are operating at a lower energy level. Be mindful of what you eat and know the better the fuel the better the results. As the old saying goes, garbage in garbage out. You get the point.

11

THE LESS I THINK, THE BETTER I DO

Thinking has always been revered in our society. We praise those who are described as great thinkers. Most people were taught to think and not feel. When a problem arises, we are conditioned to try to solve it. This is generally accomplished by mentally figuring out what to do. There are many methods to be employed when attempting to solve a problem, most of which require serious brain work.

As natural problem solvers, human beings believe they can use their superior intellect to overcome any obstacle. Although this technique can be very successful in some cases, it can be extremely detrimental in others. Thinking, like anything else in life, has both benefits and shortcomings. When thinking becomes our only source of intelligence, we lose our intuitive edge. Too much thinking will block your natural flow of ideas and your inherent connection to the unlimited power of the universe.

Your level of thinking, or how much you think, is based on the amount of control you desire to maintain. People who are always trying to control their environment are engaged in constant thinking and scheming. They are in a state of panic as they attempt to keep tabs on everyone and everything around them. As you can imagine, this is very exhausting behavior that creates a tremendous amount of stress. This behavior is based on deep insecurity and fear.

Your individual level of thinking was established as you were growing up. If you grew up in a hostile emotional environment, it may have been necessary to shut your feelings down. This may have been the best method available to protect you emotionally. Human beings are designed to make adjustments that will help them survive. This happens physically and emotionally. A carpenter may develop a callous on his hand to protect it from injury. Similarly, we use thinking and logic to create an emotional callous to protect us from deeper, more painful feelings. In some cases, your intellect is all you have to help you survive and protect you from harm.

The emotional conditioning we received early in life stays with us. Constant overthinking is one of the protective patterns we develop to help us survive. This is not something that can simply be turned on and off like a light switch. Once you are shut down emotionally, it is very difficult to reconnect to your feelings. Many people I work with tell me they cannot feel anything.

Sue was continually being abused emotionally by her demanding boss. It did not matter to him that she was a top producer. Every time she talked to him, he would point out what she was doing wrong. Sue never reacted to any of these comments or slurs. It was as if she was unable to feel the pain he was dishing out.

This was a survival skill she had developed as a child. Her mother had treated her with the same insensitivity and cruelty. To defend herself against these attacks, Sue shut her feelings off. She was well-equipped to deal with the tirades of her boss. As you know by now, Sue attracted this type of boss based on her vibration of energy. The boss was a stand-in for her mother and treated her exactly the same way.

Instead of feeling the pain caused by these attacks, Sue rationalized her boss's behavior. "He doesn't really mean it," and, "That's just the way he communicates," were common responses. Sue had lost her ability to feel the pain. In some cases, this can be helpful, but there are many disastrous side effects. This lack of feeling carried over into all of Sue's relationships. She struggled in her relationships with friends, coworkers, and men as a result.

OVERTHINKING BLOCKS FEELINGS AND ENERGY

Too much thinking blocks your true feelings and does not allow you to clear negative patterns of behavior. The only way to change your energy vibration is to feel. When you are thinking too much, it is not possible to feel. The overthinking that people engage in is designed to keep them from feeling their feelings. This is how the ego remains in control.

The conviction that you can always figure everything out is the ultimate victory for the ego. You must relinquish the desire to control to truly be free. In one of my favorite songs, Sting says, "If you love someone set them free." By setting others free you are releasing your own burdens. This is connected to the feelings of trust discussed earlier.

Thinking is also a catalyst for worry and fear. When you are flowing you are not thinking. The minute you begin to think, you start to see what can go wrong. You have now changed your focus from the goal to the manufactured obstacle.

All great entrepreneurs are very good at remaining focused on their goals. They are not thinking about debt, bills, or issues with contractors. The only thing on their minds is to complete the mission. Walt Disney faced a multitude of problems when he was building Disneyland. There were money concerns, union problems, and mechanical issues. When the park first opened, many of the rides did not function properly. That did not matter to Walt because he was focused on the ultimate goal.

HELP IS ALWAYS THERE FOR YOU

The universe wants to help you on every step of your journey. When you are locked into your purpose, you are vibrating high energy. You see only the target, and you are not encumbered by the nonsense of the outside world. When you are in this state of feeling, everything you need will come to you. The right people will appear to assist you, unexpected money will arrive exactly when needed, and ideas will flow like water.

You are now in a state of feeling and flow. This is the ultimate place to strive for in the world we live in. When you achieve this feeling, you experience a state of transcendence. You have moved into a trancelike feeling of unlimited energy. At this point, you are connected to source energy and allowing the universe to help you with every step of your journey.

If you revert to thinking again, you move into doubt and fear. Then you start to depend on logic, and suddenly problems begin to arise. The good fortune and flow you were feeling suddenly comes to a grinding halt. Even people who are highly skilled at staying in the flow state slip back occasionally. Eventually, you will be able to limit your thinking and remain connected to the universe.

Ultimately this is all about getting out of your own way. We all tend to make life difficult by trying to manipulate and control as much as possible. Life is much easier when you let go and enjoy the ride. I am asking you to have faith once again.

As you can see, this is a recurring theme. This is a very difficult issue for all of us, and it takes time to gain comfort with this approach. When you see yourself slipping into overthinking mode, it is important to be aware and stop. The doom-and-gloom, overthinking train can pick up steam very fast. Stop whatever you are doing and refocus on your goal. As you do this, you will reenergize the feeling of joy that is driving you forward. Following your true path is a celebration of your soul. Maintain that feeling and let the universe set the course.

Stop attempting to figure everything out all the time. It is completely unnecessary, and not required for you to move forward. Your job is not to manipulate every aspect of life and business. All you have to do is stop thinking long enough to see the right road.

STAYING IN FEELING

Connecting to your feelings and not trying to intellectually problem-solve will take practice. You have been conditioned to move directly into thinking mode. Now I am telling you to feel things as they happen. It is natural to resist feelings because of your old conditioning. There is a fear that by opening up your feelings you will become vulnerable and weak. Nothing could be further from the truth. You gain power when you become attuned to how you feel.

The next time something happens, pay attention to how it is making you feel. You may react strongly to an incident or a particular person. Feelings of anger or strong desires are triggers for the deeper feelings you must experience. If you are angry, which is a surface emotion, there is a deeper, more powerful feeling you are moving toward. If you do not resolve this deeper emotional issue, it is sure to resurface in your life.

There is a common misconception regarding emotional people. If someone is very emotional, it does not necessarily mean they are feeling their emotions. Many people use drama to hide from their true feelings. You probably know plenty of folks who are constantly crying and being overly dramatic. This is a great way to elicit sympathy and avoid the issue at hand. Do not confuse drama with a true connection to emotions.

There are certain circumstances in which it will be difficult to feel your emotions on the spot. You may be in a meeting or seeing a client when a feeling emerges. In this case, it is best to notice what is happening from an emotional standpoint. Later in the day, you can mentally re-create the situation in your mind. This will help you reconnect to the emotion you were feeling at that moment and gain some understanding.

I remember a client describing such a situation as he was presenting it to a potentially large client. Andrew felt that the prospect, a corporate vice president, did not give him the respect and time he required to present his program. I asked him how the potential client made him *feel*. His first response was raw anger. As we delved deeper into his feelings, he realized the client was bringing up the same feelings as his father. Andrew's father never paid enough attention to him or made him feel special.

The vice president represented an authority figure to Andrew. He evoked in him the same feeling that Andrew had been repressing for years. Once Andrew owned the feeling of disrespect he originally felt from his father, he was able to clear the negative energy and stop re-creating this type of situation.

We are constantly creating these situations in order to help us resolve the issues we came here to conquer. These incidents are a manifestation of the unconscious energy we are vibrating. No matter what happens, it is important to remember that *you* created the situation. This is a difficult concept to admit and embrace at first. In time it will become your automatic reaction to all incidents and issues in your life.

YOUR ENERGY METER

In the world of energy, you can only be doing one of two things. You are either flowing with or blocking your energy. This creates a positive or negative vibration of energy, which will attract accordingly. Your job is to remain in a state of flow as often as possible. The longer you remain in this state, the easier things will be in your life. The more you resist and block, the harder life will become. Use the chart in Figure 11.1 to monitor your feelings daily. When your internal experience matches the left side of the chart, you are flowing. If you slide to the right, you are blocking.

Flowing Energy	Blocking Energy
Acceptance	Resistance
Love	Fear/Guilt
Gratitude	Lack
Truth	Denial

FIGURE 11.1 Energy Meter Chart

At first glance, this little chart may seem simplistic. A deeper review will bring many of your patterns of behavior and feelings to the surface. Monitor yourself throughout the day and see how you are doing. You may be surprised at how much time you spend on the right (blocking) side of the chart. As you become more aware of your feelings it will become easier to remain on the left (flowing) side of the chart.

The more time you spend flowing, the easier your life will become. Remaining in a constant state of flow is more difficult than it may appear. There are many challenges and obstacles that arise to test your resolve daily. In any situation, you always have a choice of flowing or blocking. If you begin to justify negative behavior, you will become trapped in a negative energy vibration. Remain true to your feelings and let the energy flow.

PART TWO

YOUR STRATEGY

12

DEFINING YOUR MISSION

The Blues Brothers were "on a mission from God," and so are you. You came to this planet for a specific purpose. In using the word mission, I'm referring to what your business, product, or service is here to accomplish. The successful people I know are not just trying to sell something—they are on a mission. It is not simply about making a sale as much as it is about elevating others. When you make a sale, the product or service you sell should bring the recipient to a higher level of energy vibration. Your objective is to help amplify the energy of others with every sale.

Walt Disney's vision was to create a theme park, a place where people could live out their fantasies. Disney was not worried about the sale. He focused on the product he was creating. He was not worried about the investors or the profit and loss statement. He was too locked into his vision to worry about trivial issues such as money and profit.

The moment you enter the gates of Disneyland in California or of Walt Disney World in Florida, you feel better. Your energy is immediately jolted to a higher level. That feeling is exactly what Walt had in mind when he conceived the idea for the parks. Millions of people flock there every year to feel that energy.

These people are attracted to the energy vibrating from these amazing locations. It has nothing to do with the rides or characters—it's the feeling. This is a very difficult concept for salespeople to grasp. Focus on the mission, not the money.

Google founders Sergey Brin and Larry Page explained their lofty ambitions. "Searching and organizing all the world's information is an unusually important task that should be carried out by a company that is trustworthy and interested in the public good," they wrote in an unprecedented letter to the *Wall Street Journal*. This is what having a mission is about.

Google became the most popular destination on the Internet based on the feeling experienced by users. This feeling spread from one person to the next, starting a chain reaction. The momentum of positive energy is impossible to stop. Once again, the creators were more interested in the mission. They wanted to create something others would enjoy using. Pure intentions translate into unlimited success.

Think about why your product or service is here and how it can benefit others. This is how successful people create great wealth. When you are only concerned with sales numbers, you lose sight of the real issue. The key to your success is having something that will make this world a better place.

It does not matter if you operate a local, regional, national, or international business. Your only concern should be to make your piece of the world better for others. When you adopt this philosophy, your energy will change, and that positive energy will affect others. As you begin to emit this feeling to others, you become contagious.

Describe your mission in crystal clear terms. I like to think of this as painting your picture. See exactly what you want to create and add as much detail as possible. Every great accomplishment in the world started as an idea. The world we live in was created by thought. Our thoughts carry energy that is sent to the universe. When you maintain the energy, the idea begins to manifest in the physical world.

Great ideas are driven by pure thoughts that are flowing through you. These are not thoughts designed to manipulate or control. This is the difference between negative thinking and a positive flow of thoughtful energy.

Your ideas are connected to your dreams and desires. All these thoughts are designed to help you express yourself in this world. When you ignore your ideas and dreams, you are not living life to the fullest.

There are no limits in the universe. You should have a gigantic vision, mission, and purpose. If you think small, you will remain that way. The universe is waiting for your big idea. Let it out and share it with the world!

GENERATING REVENUE WITH PURPOSE

Building your income or business is not only about making more sales. You must pay attention to how and where the revenue is being generated. In order to accomplish your goals, it is important to be congruent with your mission. How you grow is more important than the dollars involved. Some salespeople and organizations focus on the numbers only. This does not tell the entire story. You have to be aware of your direction and make sure this is where you want to go.

PUMPING THE NUMBERS

One of my friends was working for an Internet-based marketing company funded by venture capitalists. The goal of the owners was to drive the sales numbers and sell the company. They were not concerned with building relationships or delivering high quality. All they were interested in was showing tremendous growth each month.

The strategy was based on high commissions for the salespeople and monthly bonuses. The owners believed that all people are motivated by money and nothing else. In the beginning, the strategy was very successful. The salespeople worked hard and pumped the numbers month after month. All was well and the plan seemed to be working perfectly.

After a year of feverish activity and unmerciful pounding by the owners, the system began to crumble. Customer complaints were mounting, and orders were being canceled. Suddenly the salespeople were no longer receiving their high commissions and bonuses. The true intention and energy of the owners had surfaced and manifested accordingly.

When an organization is based solely on numbers it is doomed to failure. The universe cannot be fooled by a slick business plan and a platinum card. All organizations are living organisms. The collective energy of a group of people can move mountains or tear down great accomplishments. Be aware of your feelings when selling your product or service. Are you coming to help or is it all about the numbers?

Figure 12.1 is an example of a revenue source report. The first three columns are defined as follows:

Revenue Source: How revenue is generated.

Percent of Total Revenue: The percentage of the company's total revenue derived in each category.

Average Sales $ per Client/Year: The amount of money each client spends per year.

Revenue Source	Percent of Total Revenue	Average Sales $ per Client/ Year	Total Number of Accounts/ Sales in Category	Total Sales
Consulting	33	5,000	40	330,000
Training	50	3,000	30	500,000
Product Sales	17	500	200	170,000
Total	100		270	1,000,000

FIGURE 12.1 ABC Training Company's Current Sales

In this scenario, ABC Company made a total of 270 sales to generate $1 million in total revenue. The number one revenue category for the business is training, which represented 50 percent of the company's sales.

This report is used as a map to determine if the company is moving in the right direction based on its objective and vision. If ABC Company executives are happy with this revenue breakdown, they can continue to grow the business with these percentages. On the other hand, if ABC wants to move in another direction, then revenue changes are necessary.

Let's assume that ABC's directors want to generate a total of $3 million in sales in the next five years. They also want 50 percent of revenue to be derived from product sales. Product sales currently represent only 17 percent of the company's total revenue. Adjustments will have to be made to ABC's sales philosophy to move sales in the direction of products. Figure 12.2 shows how the revenue source report will change in the next five years.

Revenue Source	Percent of Total Revenue	Average Sales $ per Client/ Year	Total Number of Accounts/ Sales in Category	Total Sales
Consulting	16	5,000	100	500,000
Training	34	3,000	333.3	1,000,000
Product Sales	50	500	3,000	1,500,000
Total	100		270	3,000,000

FIGURE 12.2 ABC Training Company's Sales in Five Years

The big change here is in how the revenue is generated. Growing your business is not about revenue alone. The way you generate revenue is equally important. You have to grow your business based on how you want to evolve in the future. Do not focus on revenue alone when determining your definition of success.

ADDITIONAL REVENUE STREAMS

You should also be thinking about additional ways to generate revenue. When I started my business, my only source of revenue was conducting seminars. Then I added training, consulting, and products. This allowed me to dramatically increase my revenue base. I was able to sell multiple products and services to my existing clients. By doing so, I added more revenue without adding new clients. Additional services and products are a great way to add dollars with limited effort.

Look at your business and think about the products and services you can add. Set up a schedule and plan when you will introduce each new item. I would like to add four to six new products and seminars per year. New information gives people a reason to continue to work with you. It is also a great way to reconnect with clients you may have lost contact with over the years.

Many ideas in this area are stimulated by your existing clients. You may hear a few different clients express problems in a particular area. This is an opportunity for you to create an additional product or service that can fill this need. The more options you offer a client the better your odds of making a sale.

I was working with a company that offers training for people who are interested in becoming matchmakers. The only service they offered was a one-time weekend training. After the training was completed, there was nothing else the clients could purchase from the company.

Several of the students were interested in marketing help, especially on the Internet. This created several opportunities, including the development of a lead generation website and a template for new graduates to use when they start. Members are required to pay a monthly fee to use the website and receive leads from interested parties. The next project on the table is additional training materials that students may purchase before or after attending the training.

There are countless opportunities to add new products or services for your clients. All you have to do is pay attention to their needs. Look for problems to solve or holes to fill, and a new revenue category will be created. If you add a few new products or services each year, it will dramatically increase your bottom line and make a lot of people very happy.

13

THE BRAND AND YOU

The world has become brand crazy. People have strong loyalty to the brands they buy and use on a regular basis. Each year thousands of new products are tested and millions of dollars are spent. In the end, a very small percentage of these products ever reach the shelves of your favorite store. Think about your last trip to the supermarket. When you look at your cart, I am sure you always see the same items, demonstrating your own brand loyalty.

The product or service you sell is a brand. Your prospects and customers make an emotional connection to what you sell. This is where brand loyalty begins for the consumer. It is the emotional connection that keeps the customer coming back.

Think about your emotional association with the following brands. Write down the first thing that comes into your mind when you think about these popular brands.

Starbucks
Walmart
Tiffany
McDonald's
Target
Rolex

Calvin Klein

As you can see, you have a feeling or emotional connection to all of these brands. Certain feelings arise at the mere mention of the name. Your product or service is no different. The second a customer thinks of your product or service, they get a feeling. Are they getting the feeling you want them to have? I would suggest asking your clients this question: "What is the first feeling that comes up when you think of our product/service?"

The answer to this simple question will tell you a lot about how you are doing in the market. Are people viewing your product or service in a way that makes you happy? You may be very surprised at the answers you receive when asking this question. Do not assume you are projecting the image you desire to the marketplace.

Ask yourself, "How do I want people to feel when they think about my product/service?" In many cases, people are so concerned with selling that they lose sight of the image they are projecting. Do not underestimate the power of the emotional connection to a brand. If you doubt the strength of this loyalty, ask someone to change brands for one of their favorite items. You may be surprised at how fiercely loyal consumers can be.

YOU, TOO, ARE A BRAND

Your product or service is not the only brand in the game. You are what I like to call a *personal brand*. Others see you a certain way—that is your personal brand. Personal brands are very clear when we think about actors. Most actors have a specific brand attached to their names. What do you think of when you see the following names?

Sylvester Stallone
Brad Pitt
Jennifer Lopez
Jim Carrey
Robert De Niro

Julia Roberts

When you think of Sylvester Stallone, I am quite sure you think of action. Stallone is synonymous with characters such as Rocky and Rambo. Many years ago, Sly took a shot at comedy in the film *Oscar*. The bottom line was simply this: People do not see Stallone as a funny guy. No matter what he does, all we see is Rocky or Rambo—his brand.

Something interesting happened at several of my live seminars when I mentioned Brad Pitt. More than half of the audience thought of Angelina Jolie. That is not a very good job of branding for Mr. Pitt. This also shows the power of association. If you become connected with another brand, you may lose your own identity and strength in the market.

All these people are also attached to an image. Are you projecting the image you want the client to feel? An emotional connection has been made between you and the client. Have you created the connection you really want?

Years ago, I was working for a local shopper publication called *Pennysaver*. One day one of the sales reps came in saying, "I hate that every time I walk into a client the people say 'Here comes the Pennysaver Lady.'" I told her that *she* had created the brand and that it could be changed. In time she changed that perception.

Branding is a big part of sales because people become comfortable with and loyal to brands, they trust. To be successful you must become the brand of choice in your category of business. Make sure you pay close attention to the feelings and connections you are building relative to your brand. They will be great assets— or liabilities.

GOING TOO WIDE

Another major challenge facing businesses today is establishing a brand within a niche. The most successful companies and salespeople have created a niche for themselves. Once you select your niche, you can begin to establish yourself within that market.

There are many variables when selecting a niche market. In more specialized selling, your niche can be extremely focused. You may be selling exclusively to attorneys, chiropractors, hospitals, or auto dealers. The next level is the niche within a niche. You could be selling only to attorneys who earn over $250,000 per year and have offices in Manhattan.

Many companies and salespeople fear the niche approach. They worry that there may not be enough prospects in the market to make money. The reality is the complete opposite. It is much more difficult to attempt to sell to the entire world than to a specific niche.

One of the keys to success is being known as a specialist. I know many marketing professionals attempting to offer a laundry list of services. These so-called marketing experts are having trouble establishing a client base. Then we have the marketing pros who realize the importance of specialization. The top marketing experts in the world are known for a specific area of expertise. They may be experts in Internet marketing, copywriting, direct mail, or television advertising. If you need copywriting, you would seek out an expert in that field. It would not make sense to look for a general marketing company.

When I mentioned the title of this book to people, several of them told me I should change it. They felt the title *Spiritual Selling* would turn too many people off. By contrast, I felt it gave me a specific brand and position in the market. Instead of being just another sales trainer, I was "the Spiritual Sales Trainer." No one else is branding themselves in that manner. This gives me a distinct brand in a crowded market category.

Do not be afraid to be different or controversial. When you are like everyone else, you blend into the pack. Top sellers want to be noticed and remembered. Anyone can be safe and make a living. Dare to be different and make an impression no one will ever forget.

COLORS ELICIT FEELINGS

Companies spend a fortune building brands, creating logos, and selecting colors. Each color has a specific feeling attached to it. All colors represent different things to specific groups of people. It is for this reason that the colors you select to represent you are so important.

If I asked you the color of a can of Coke, you would quickly say red. How about Pepsi (blue) or Sprite (green)? These images come into your mind immediately. Sprite followed the same color scheme as another successful lemon-lime soda, 7UP. The market was already conditioned to the green cans associated with that flavor.

The same thing happened with Snack Wells. When these low-fat cookies (an oxymoron to me) were introduced, the boxes were green. The minute you walked down the cookie aisle and saw the green boxes, you knew you were in the low-fat section. Green is associated with health, so it was a great choice for a low-fat product. Soon after that, low-fat Pop-Tarts were introduced. Guess what? That box was green, too. Why reinvent the wheel when the market has already been conditioned to green, meaning low-fat?

Pay attention to these trends in the market. People are constantly being conditioned to associate colors with products and feelings. Most of the generic colas in the supermarket are in red cans. People associate red cans with Coke, so this is a natural choice.

You may be able to apply this strategy to your business. If a major corporation has spent millions conditioning the public, your colors can dovetail with those that are already well recognized. Use the same colors as a major corporation to elicit the exact feeling in your clients. The only difference now between you and the major company is that you did not spend the money conditioning the market.

Color Chart		
Color	Associated with	Preferred by
Red	Blood, fire, competition, heat, emotion, optimism, violence, communism	Achievers, active women, most economically stable, most secure
Orange	Extroversion, adventure, celebration	Adolescents, bright orange is the second least favorite color overall
Yellow	Sunshine, creativity, imagination, optimism, futuristic, spirituality, low prices	The first color kids reach for, yet the least preferred overall color
Green	Ecology, nature, balance, envy, spring	Opinion leaders, trendsetters
Blue	Dependability, water, sky, holiness, loyalty, patience, hope, sadness	No. 1 favorite color in America
Purple/ Violet	Passion, spirituality, art, creativity, wit, sensitivity, vanity, royalty	No. 3 favorite, popular among 18- to 29-year- olds, artists, loved or hated more than any other color
Pink	Romance, sweetness, delicacy, tenderness, refinement, femininity	Women
Brown	Earth, substance, harmony, home, stability	Practical people, down-to- earth people
Black	Sophistication, simplicity, death and mourning, bad luck, night, power	Intellectuals, rebels, fashion industry, increasingly broad appeal
Gray	Neutrality, boredom, coolness, conservatism	Not generally chosen as a favorite, usually not a big seller
White	Purity, sterility, calm, mourning	Intellectuals, modern types, limited appeal overall

FIGURE 13.1 Chart of Color Associations Use the chart in Figure 13.1 to evaluate your color choices.

CREATING A CLIENT PROFILE

Understanding your client is critical to your success. The key in this area is to create a profile of the perfect client for your business. In this case, I invoke the 80 percent rule. This rule states that 80 percent of your business comes from a specific client type. You will always have clients on either side of the profile, but they are not the people you are targeting.

One of my clients offers technical support to small businesses. His target client is a small business with ten to fifty employees with revenues from $1 million to $5 million. His company supports only service businesses specializing in marketing, as well as design firms.

In the business-to-business arena, your profile has two levels. The first level is the type of businesses you sell to or the niche. The second level is the type of person who makes the buying decision. When you do a good job of targeting your customer, you will find that the same type of person is usually making the decisions.

If you sell to the public, the same rules apply. You must create a targeted client profile. A women's clothing store may target twenty-eight- to thirty-five-year-old women with an annual income of $50,000 to $75,000. The key here is to adjust the numbers to make them as tight as possible. If you said your target was women ages eighteen to thirty-eight, it would be much more difficult to create a sales strategy. An eighteen-year-old is completely different from a thirty-eight-year-old. What motivates one does not attract the other. Our example of twenty-eight- to thirty-five-year-old women makes a lot more sense. Now all of your sales and marketing strategies can revolve around the target client.

Use the following profile form to paint a picture of your perfect client. Use the 80 percent rule when going through this exercise. Do not concern yourself with the people on either side of the profile. You will always have a percentage of sales outside the target. We are only interested in speaking to the bread-and-butter clients responsible for 80 percent of your revenue.

Business Type: _____ Size: _____ Revenue: _____
Age (within 10-15 years, such as 25-35): _____
Male (%): _____
Female(%): _____
Income (within $25,000, such as $75,000-$100,000): _____
Married or single: _____
Children: _____
White collar or blue collar: _____
Homeowners (%): _____
Rent (%): _____
Local (%): _____
Regional (%): _____
National(%): _____
International (%): _____
Leisure activites: _____
Type of car: _____
Coffee or tea drinker: _____
Favorite foods: _____
Sports they like and play: _____
Teams they like: _____

Client Profile (Your Ideal Client)

KNOW YOUR CUSTOMER BETTER THAN YOU KNOW YOURSELF

Sales organizations spend the majority of their time focusing on tactics and techniques designed to close a deal. Most of this revolves around what the salesperson is going to do to get the client to buy. This relates back to the predator mentality I spoke of earlier.

The Attractor Sales Process™ revolves around the customer. If you have a greater understanding of what the customer wants, you have a much better chance of making the sale. This strategy involves filling a need you know the customer has to fill instead of arbitrarily trying to sell something. This is a much easier and less stressful approach.

Spend as much time as possible getting inside the head of your customers. You have to know how they think and what is important to them. Understand their emotional makeup and what drives them. As with any successful relationship in life, the more I understand your needs, the better our relationship will be.

MAKING AN EMOTIONAL INVESTMENT

Successful selling revolves around the level of emotional investment made by the salesperson and the prospect. This is no different than the dynamic in a romantic relationship. Both parties must be emotionally invested for the relationship to flourish. Salespeople tend to see clients as notches on their belts. In some ways, this mirrors the behavior of men who see women as conquests. The belief in this mindset is that the more notches I have, the better I am.

When people are emotionally invested in something, they are more interested and attentive. I have seen many cases where a sale is made, and the prospect does not even know what they have actually purchased. Regardless of how hard you try, there will always be people not willing to make this emotional commitment. This is starting to sound a lot like dating—and it is.

The emotional investment begins with the salesperson's level of energy and commitment. If the salesperson is not emotionally involved, you cannot expect the prospect to get excited. The prospect will feel your energy immediately. They will feel attracted or repulsed based on the energy you are vibrating.

When the salesperson is emotionally charged, that is the energy the prospect feels. The same thing happens when you meet someone you are attracted to romantically. They feel your energy and know you are interested in them. In sales, the prospect must feel you are interested in their needs. This is the first step in establishing an emotional connection.

The energy of the relationship is elevated when both parties are investing equally. Once this investment has been made, a bond forms between the two parties. Now both people are putting energy into the relationship. The ultimate goal in this scenario is a favorable result for both participants. There is no winning or losing in this case. This is the difference when an emotional investment is at the core of the relationship.

It is important to focus your energy on engaging people in the sales process. I love people who ask a lot of questions. This is a sure sign the person is engaged in what you are saying. Some of these people may seem to be difficult to deal with. In most cases, these will become your most loyal clients and the best source of referrals. I saw the power of emotional investment when I met the head of a networking organization to whom I had been referred for a speaking engagement. His name was John, and one of his members had referred me. We scheduled a telephone call to discuss the event and my topic.

I was to offer a forty-five-minute presentation to approximately one hundred of his top members. John grilled me with questions, reviewed my website, and asked me to send him a DVD (back when people watched DVDs). My first thought was, "Wow, this guy is really intense for a forty-five-minute presentation to his networking group." We spoke again and exchanged several e-mails before agreeing to a date.

When I arrived, it was obvious to me that this was going to be a great presentation. I could see the excitement in the audience and knew they were emotionally charged. It was one of the best audiences I had ever encountered.

After the meeting, I spoke with John about his vigilance in booking our date. He told me that it was extremely important to him not to waste his members' time. John was emotionally invested in his buying decision. We are still working together, and I always appreciate his level of commitment.

ARE YOU A FISH OR DUCK?

Every successful entrepreneur and salesperson understands his market category and pricing model. You must remain true to your category to gain market share and build a strong identity (brand). A fish is a fish, and a duck is a duck. If a fish tried to be a duck, he would fail miserably.

The third-generation owner of a hardware store in my neighborhood has been able to grow his business in an environment dominated by mega-stores like Home Depot and Lowe's. I asked him, "How are you able to compete with this type of store?" His answer: "I do not try to compete with those guys. That would be a losing approach for me." He knows that he is a fish, and he does not attempt to look like a duck. People would see through that immediately. One of his employees told me, "Home Depot sells paint cheaper than we can buy it." They only stock paint as a convenience for the customer, and they sell more of it than you would think. The entire business is built around specialty items and superior service. If you need a screw for the back of your screen door that has a flat head and is a certain diameter, they have it. As a matter of fact, one of the people on the floor will take the time to help you find that exact twenty-five-cent screw. An employee at a mega-store would never take the time to help a customer find a twenty-five-cent item.

Knowing who you are and what you can and cannot do will be a great asset to your success. Do not get into a fight, you know you cannot win. Trying to compete with mega-stores would be certain doom for this local hardware store.

Defining exactly what you are and being the best in that category is important. Make good choices and know yourself. If you are a fish, be the best fish you can be. Let the duck have his business, and you keep yours.

Much of this philosophy is related to understanding yourself. If you are a fish, you should be proud of that fact. Too many people are attempting to remold themselves based on the opinions and visions of others. The most successful people in the world are those who understand and accept themselves. Be proud of who you are and what you sell. There is no reason to hide or justify. As you gain more comfort with yourself, your energy vibration becomes more powerful.

WHAT TYPE OF PURCHASE IS YOUR PRODUCT OR SERVICE?

Every purchase will fall into a specific category based on a number of factors, including the person spending the money. When you are selling, it is important to understand the type of purchase your prospect is making. Most products or services fall into one of four categories:

1. Luxury.
2. Necessity.
3. Functional item.
4. Improvement.

Every time people make a purchase, they mentally plug it into a category. This category changes from person to person. What you sell is not as important as the perception of the buyer. Understanding this perception makes you a much more effective salesperson.

Let's say you are selling Rolex watches, for example. Rolex is a true luxury brand in the marketplace. They have spent many years establishing themselves as one of the premier brands in the watch category. When considering watches, you probably think of Rolex as a luxury purchase 100 percent of the time. If this was your belief, you would see every sale as a luxury purchase and plan an appropriate strategy.

But if we look at various sales throughout the company, our perceptions may change. When a very wealthy gentleman comes in to purchase his tenth Rolex, is it really a luxury purchase? Perhaps the man has a huge ego and wants to show off his new Rolex to other business associates or members of his country club. In this case, it is a necessity purchase based on this customer's need. He requires this new watch to fill an emotional need for his ego. This buyer does not see this as a luxury purchase. This kind of scenario is common in the luxury market. Many of the purchases are made to impress others, and in the mind of the buyer, these are not luxury purchases.

However, a person coming in for his first Rolex would see the purchase as a great luxury. This is why understanding the individual customer becomes so important. Do not make assumptions based on the type of item or price point. What is a luxury to one person is a necessity to another. Every customer is different and has unique motivators. Understanding the emotional needs and feelings of each individual you encounter will help you become much more effective.

All purchases are emotionally based. Your ability to understand the emotion driving the buyer will be a great asset to you. This will help you gain deeper insight and become a more intuitive seller. You will connect with the buyer on a much deeper level when you truly understand what is motivating them on an emotional level. Then you can help them make the best purchase based on their individual needs.

PRICING DETERMINES MARKET POSITION

Creating and remaining true to your pricing structure is critical to the establishment of your brand category. This is extremely important in the service industry where pricing is based on market perception. Understand where you are in the market and stay there. You cannot be high-end on Monday and low-end on Friday. Decide and stick with it.

You determine your pricing structure based on your brand identity and market position. It is important to establish yourself in a niche market at a certain level. Much of this perception is determined by your pricing model. Consider the advantages and disadvantages of the various pricing options.

PRICING OPTIONS

High-end: Expensive, luxury, limited client base.

Middle-market: Targeted to the full range of the middle market. This includes upper and lower-middle-class consumers or businesses.

Low-end: Mass appeal, the largest market sector. Inexpensive products or services targeted to the masses.

HIGH-END ADVANTAGES

- » Fewer transactions required, generating higher sales volume.
- » Easier to market, due to the limited number of people and businesses in the category.
- » Have more disposable income to spend.

HIGH-END DISADVANTAGES

- » Fewer potential customers, due to smaller market size.
- » A more difficult market to break into.

MIDDLE-MARKET ADVANTAGES

- » Large base to draw upon.
- » Generates solid income/revenue.
- » May offer competition to the high-end market.

MIDDLE-MARKET DISADVANTAGES

- » Hard to target specific segment.
- » Less disposable cash.

LOW-END ADVANTAGES

- » Gigantic market.
- » Always consistent in any economy.
- » Grows in a weak economy.

LOW-END DISADVANTAGES

» Large volume needed to generate revenue.
» More transactions required than any other market.
» Requires more organization and tracking, due to high volume.

DESIGNING A WINNING BENEFIT STATEMENT

Are you boring? No one wants to think they are boring, but my experience at networking events and business functions tells me most people are in fact boring. In some cases, they are extremely boring. If you ask the average person what they do for a living, you will hear an answer like "I am an accountant, computer consultant, financial planner," and so on. This does not mean anything to the prospect because they have already met hundreds of people who say the same thing. How does the average consumer know what makes you better than the next person providing the same service?

A benefit statement is designed to help you separate yourself from the crowd and make an impression. Would you rather be boring or memorable? The benefit statement is not to be confused with the dreaded *elevator speech*. I am not interested in hearing a speech of any kind, especially from someone I do not know. A benefit statement is a quick-hitting strategy designed to get people's attention and interest. A solid benefit statement will help you dramatically increase lead flow and generate tremendous interest in your product or service. Your benefit statement describes what you do. There are two main problems I see with most benefit statements:

1. The statement is too long and boring (the speech).
2. The statement doesn't spell out a benefit.

Saying things like "We have the best price and service" is so clichéd it's painful to hear. Most people are boring because they are afraid to make powerful, definitive statements.

Top producers exude confidence and know they are the best. This creates a very attractive vibration of energy that draws people in. You must not be fearful in the sales game. You must project the confidence to achieve the level of success you desire.

Your job is to convey a strong benefit in one sentence that makes the prospect say, "How do you do that?" You will know your statement works when people start asking that question.

I am a sales and marketing expert, but no one cares about that fact. There are plenty of sales and marketing experts in the world. My job is to distinguish myself by making a strong benefit statement. So if I am attending a small business event and someone asks me what I do, I say, "I help small business owners double their sales in the next twelve months or less using the Attractor System." This statement always gets the "How do you do that?" response from a potential client.

This is how you move the prospect into your sales process. (The actual sales process is outlined later in this book.) Having a powerful benefit statement will dramatically increase the number of qualified leads you generate. This one simple adjustment has transformed the businesses of many of my clients.

Let's break down the elements of this statement. This will make it easier for you to construct a great benefit statement of your own.

PART 1: QUALIFYING

"I help small business owners . . ." Targeting the statement helps you eliminate people who are not right for your business. One of my clients sells to architects only. We open his statement with, "I specialize in helping architects." Do not fear excluding people when you deliver your statement. Your goal is to immediately eliminate people who are not right for your product or service. If you are selling to architects and I am a dentist, why would you want to tell me your story?

Many entrepreneurs and salespeople fear this specialization, thinking that narrowing the market too much is a negative approach. The reality is that the more specialized you are, the more powerful the statement can be. You do not want to waste time speaking to people who will never buy from you. I would rather know immediately and move on to the next prospect. Time is a valuable asset and there is none to waste.

PART 2: BENEFIT

". . . double their sales in the next twelve months or less . . ." There are two important elements of the benefit:

1. Bottom line benefit (double sales).
2. The timeline (next twelve months or less).

People want to know what you will do for them and how long it will take to accomplish. The key here is remembering that the benefit is for them. Prospects get excited when they feel you can help them do something more efficiently. The elements of speed and increased levels of success are tremendous motivators. If you watch infomercials, especially about weight loss, you will see this formula over and over again. One of my clients in the physical fitness field used the statement, "The miracle diet and exercise program." This was not an effective statement, because it lacked exact benefit and timeline. We changed it to "Lose ten pounds in fourteen days with the miracle diet program." This change tripled his response rates. The more detail you can give, the more powerful the statement will be.

The use of numbers and percentages is also very effective. The human mind reacts much better to exact numbers. This technique also helps the prospect frame the benefit in exact terms. When you tell someone they can lose fourteen pounds in ten days, it creates a powerful mental image.

PART 3: HOW

". . . using the Attractor Sales System." The "how" is an optional part of the statement. I could end with, "Double your sales in the next twelve months or less," but adding the "how" gives it more depth. The statement now feels complete to the prospect because it names the method, I use to help increase sales. Although it does not spell out what the system is or how it works, it implies process.

Words such as *system*, *process*, and *plan* are associated with structure and imply know-how in a specific area. Buyers want to know that you have a proven track record. These words help assure the prospect that you know how to assist them in achieving their goals.

CREDIBILITY STATEMENT

The second type of benefit statement is credibility driven. This style is more effective when you know you are speaking to your target audience. It is less aggressive and more engaging when a higher level of trust is required. This concern applies to people in the financial sector and insurance, for example. By establishing credibility, you create a stronger image for yourself as the seller.

One of my clients in the graphic design business uses this statement: "We are an award-winning graphic design firm specializing in getting your business noticed." Again, let's examine the elements of this statement.

PART 1: CREDIBILITY

"We are an award winning . . ." Winning awards builds your image and credibility immediately. People in certain industries like knowing you have attained a level of recognition. Credibility can also be conveyed by the number of years you have been in business or by mentioning some of your top clients.

PART 2: WHAT YOU DO

" . . . graphic design firm . . ." This part of the statement tells the prospect exactly what service you provide. This is like the "qualifying" part of the benefit statement we examined earlier. If the prospect is not interested in your service, you will know immediately.

The more specific you can be, the better. If you are an Internet marketing specialist, don't tell people you are a marketing specialist. Remember, the more specific the skill, the more you can charge based on your expertise.

PART 3: BENEFIT

". . . specializing in getting your business noticed." In this example the benefit comes in at the end. It tells the prospect in a subtler manner what you will do for them. It is not as powerful as "double your sales" or "lose ten pounds in fourteen days," but it is effective in the proper environment. In some business environments, an understated benefit is more acceptable.

YOU MUST BE COMFORTABLE

The key to your success with the benefit or credibility statement is feeling comfortable when delivering your message. You must be able to deliver this statement with complete confidence and conviction. If you do not feel right when saying it, the statement will not be effective. I suggest you practice saying it to friends and colleagues before rolling it out to the market.

People will sense how comfortable you feel when delivering your statement. It's not just about the words you are saying. The feeling and energy you convey is much more important. This is no different than giving a script to two actors: One will do it well, the other will do it brilliantly. Who are you going to pay money to see?

If you feel uncomfortable delivering a powerful benefit statement, you may have another, underlying issue to deal with. That issue is fear about your skill level, product, or service. Techniques like the benefit statement only work when the person delivering the message believes in what he is saying. When fear crops up, it is important to know why you are lacking confidence. When you feel better, people will react to you in a more positive manner. The more you practice and expose your fears, the easier this will become for you.

IT'S YOUR TURN

Start writing statements using this system. Test different versions and see which one gets the best response. This is a process that will take time to perfect, so be patient. Remember, the goal of the statement is simply to pique the interest of a potential client— nothing more. It is not designed to make a sale. All you have to do is get them to say, "How do you do that?"

Work on your statement using the outlines in this section. Incorporate these elements:

- » Qualify.
- » Benefit.
- » How (optional but recommended).
- » Credibility (optional).

A solid benefit statement will dramatically increase your response rates and sales volume. Do not underestimate the value of a strong benefit statement. Continue to tweak and adjust your statement until it is perfect.

14

THE NUMBERS THAT COUNT

Most of my new clients tell me they need more business right away. They believe the key to success is getting more leads. It is the classic "It's just a numbers game" mentality. Generating more leads is important, but learning how to qualify them is critical. You do not want to waste time with prospects that are not right for your business.

When you analyze your sales figures, it is important to look beyond the numbers on a computer screen or piece of paper. There are variables that cannot be seen in the numbers alone. You must learn to see beyond the numbers and make the necessary adjustments to improve your profitability and productivity. Ultimately, your goal is to improve your closing ratio and eliminate waste. There are four key points to examine when evaluating your sales figures and forecasts:

1. Quality of leads.
2. Selling cycle.
3. Closing ratio.
4. Average sale.

QUALITY OF LEADS

How good are the leads you are generating? Pure numbers do not tell the story when evaluating your closing ratio. Are you generating high-quality leads or just volume? To be successful, it is important that the leads you generate are high quality.

Evaluate each appointment you make and determine the level of quality. I use a simple three-tier system to determine the suitability of each prospect. This is not an attempt to judge the prospect. The objective is to determine the individual's level of interest.

Level 1: High interest. This level indicates that the prospect is a very good match for your business. A Level 1 prospect will display great interest in your product or service. This person will reply to your requests for information and keep the lines of communication open. These people deserve your utmost attention and the highest level of service.

Level 2: Medium Interest. Level 2 means the prospect is potentially a good match but there are some issues to be dealt with. This level of prospect is the key to your success. While the Level 1 prospect is a very good match and has great interest, a prospect at Level 2 can be equally good but does not have the same type of interest. When you are able to convert more prospects on this level, your business begins to make leaps forward. A small increase in this area will be dramatic for your sales and revenue.

One of the traps in this category is not to waste time on those who will not buy. You must know when to stop pursuing prospects in this category. If you are not making progress, it is time to walk away.

Level 3: Low interest. These prospects are not right for your business. The best thing to do with people in this category is to walk away as soon as possible. One of the reasons salespeople struggle is they waste too much time with people who will never buy. Time is your most valuable commodity, and it must not be wasted on people in Level 3.

Place each new prospect in one of these three categories as soon as you feel you have gathered enough information. As you practice this system, you will become better at evaluating your potential new clients. This will help you develop a sixth sense regarding new business.

SELLING CYCLE

How long does it take to close a sale? Knowing your selling cycle is a great asset when forecasting your sales. The selling cycle is the time it takes from the first significant contact with a new prospect to closing the deal. If you know it takes three months to close a sale from your first contact, that is your cycle. Although each sale is unique, it is important to know your average sales cycle. One deal may take a month, another six months. The general rule is, the more expensive the purchase, the longer the cycle.

CLOSING RATIO

Another important tool in the forecasting process is the closing ratio. How many appointments does it take to make a sale? How many prospects do you have to see before one becomes a customer? If you have a 30 percent (3 out of 10) closing ratio and have a goal of 6 deals per month, you must have 20 appointments per month. Any time you fail to reach the necessary number of appointments, you will miss your goal. The closing ratio is greatly affected by the quality of lead you are generating. I have seen dramatic increases in closing ratios resulting solely from a higher quality of lead. Once again, this is not a simple numbers game.

AVERAGE SALE

Knowing your average sale is critical to proper forecasting. This is simple math but many people have no idea what this number is for them. Simply divide the total sales dollars by the number of transactions and you have your average sale. I know this seems very simple, but far too many people are not aware of this number.

The report in Figure 14.1 was used by one of my clients. When we began working together, her belief was there were not enough leads.

Month	Number of Leads	Number of Closed	Closing Ratio	Average Sale	Total Sales
January	22	4	18%	$3,000	$12,000
February	20	6	30%	$3,200	$19,200
March	30	10	33%	$3,500	$35,000
April	24	8	33%	$3,300	$26,400
May	26	11	42%	$3,500	$38,500
June	24	12	50%	$4,000	$48,000

FIGURE 14.1 Sample Evaluation: Monthly Report for a Web Designer

Sharon was running a moderately successful web site design business when we met. Her belief was based purely on the number of leads she was generating per month. She was under the impression that her closing ratio was very high. "When I get in front of someone, I close the deal," she told me. I asked Sharon if she had the numbers to back up her statement. She did not.

As she began to track the numbers, a disturbing fact emerged. Her closing ratio was terrible. In January, twenty-two leads resulted in only four sales and $12,000 in revenue. This was an 18 percent closing ratio. In some businesses that would be a great ratio, but in her business it was mediocre at best. Sharon thought her sales skills were very weak and needed drastic improvement. Certainly we can all improve our skills, but that was not her problem.

A deeper look at the situation uncovered the real problem.

Sharon was presenting her service to people who did not see the value and in many cases could not afford her prices. She had been targeting local retail business owners in her area. We immediately shifted her into service businesses with revenues of $1 million to $5 million. Within six months she experienced a dramatic change in all areas of her business.

As you can see from Figure 14.1, the number of leads was not the main factor for the dramatic sales increase. It was a combination of better lead quality, closing ratio, and average sale. In June, twenty-four leads—only two more than in January—resulted in twelve sales and $48,000 in revenue.

In many cases, the problem is not the number of leads alone. It is a combination of many factors that must be evaluated on a regular basis. Generating a higher closing ratio and average sale are the easiest ways to impact your revenue at the lowest cost. Pay attention to these numbers and adjust each month. Vigilance in this area will pay huge dividends in increased revenues.

THE THREE KEYS TO LONG-TERM SUCCESS

There are three skills that you must master in order to ensure long-term success in sales:

1. Opportunities.
2. Conversions.
3. Retention.

Opportunities

When I began my sales career, all I heard about was closing. "Close, close, close" was the creed in the predator sales environment. Later I learned that closing was the easy part of the process. The hardest thing to do was open.

You must create quality selling opportunities to increase revenue. This is accomplished by opening the doors to new prospects. People always talk about closing the deal, but you have to open before you can close.

Conversions

Once you have successfully opened, it's time to close. Opening is phase one, but converting the prospect to a client is phase two. If you cannot close the deal, all the great work you did to open is useless. This process is discussed in Chapter 11.

Retention

You have done excellent work and acquired a new client. To build the business, you must retain your client base. Everyone loses some of their base each year for various reasons. It is acceptable to lose a small percentage. However, if you take care of your clients, they will take care of you. Research has shown that it costs seven times more to acquire a new client than to retain an existing one. Your entire referral base is a product of strong retention and superb service.

BUILDING VALUE

One of the greatest mistakes salespeople make is not building enough value. When you sell a product or service, you must understand that prospects are motivated by the value you bring into their lives. It does not matter if it is a business or personal transaction. The best way to build value is to bury the prospect with benefits and intangibles. The intangibles are the added value you bring that they were not thinking about before making the purchase.

A few months ago, we were looking for a painter for our newly refinished basement. We called a few friends and asked for referrals. We received two referrals and called a third painter from an ad in a local paper. The first referred painter came in the evening. He was a bit sloppy looking and seemed a bit rushed. We went into the basement, and he walked around for approximately six minutes. Then he said, "I would say this will be about $1,200."

I asked how long it would take and when he was available to do the job. He told me he would call me the next day with those details. I never heard from him again.

Painter number two came from the ad in the paper. He drove up in a very nice truck and seemed more professional. We went downstairs and he began to ask us questions. We told him what we wanted, and he said it would cost $1,400; he could come in two weeks, and the job would take three days. Although his approach was better than the first painter, I felt something was missing.

Painter number three, another referral, was going to be our last estimate before deciding. He was the youngest of the group and was dressed neatly in jeans and a button-down shirt. As we walked down the steps, he immediately began to run his hands against the walls. "These walls will require some light sanding", he explained. He proceeded to meticulously examine every inch of the basement, looking for hidden problems and issues.

Then he began to make a series of suggestions that we should consider improving the quality of the job and adding more durability to high-traffic areas. Most of his suggestions were excellent and we would never have thought of them.

Although painter number three was the most expensive, we hired him. He did an excellent job, and we were absolutely thrilled with his work. He built superior value compared to the other two painters and offered intangible benefits the others did not.

Your ability to see issues the buyer does not see will help you build a superior level of value for your customer. Anyone can quote a job. Building value is a skill that true professionals use to enhance their value to the customer. This is not done with the intention of charging more money by adding bogus products and services. In fact, in many cases, you may be suggesting something less expensive to help the customer.

When you learn to build superior value for the customer, your price becomes irrelevant. The customer is no longer looking at the price. All they see is the value and benefit you will provide. This is the most powerful position in sales and business. Once you have established superior benefits, all other aspects of the deal are minimized. If you believe you are receiving the ultimate service and value, nothing else really matters.

UNDERSTANDING WHAT YOU SELL

What are you selling and why should I buy it from you? Can you answer this question with conviction and clarity? Most people cannot and, as a result, are unable to sell their product or service.

You must have a compelling reason for a client to choose you instead of a competitor. It does not have to be an earth-shattering reason. A simple distinction can be the difference between you and another business. Why do people spend more money on FedEx when they can get the same service for less money from another carrier? The answer is peace of mind. FedEx has created that advantage and, as a result, they can charge higher rates.

When you hand your package to a FedEx driver, you never think about it again. At no time do you ever wonder if the package will be delivered safely. Building that level of trust is an incredible accomplishment for any company.

The sale is not about the product or service. This is an aspect of sales that most people miss. In reality, the sale is about the emotional connection made to your product or service. You are not selling the item—you are selling the feeling. Once this connection has been established, it is incredibly powerful in the mind of the consumer.

What are the following companies really selling?

McDonald's

Mercedes Benz

Home Depot

You

You may think McDonald's is selling fast food but, more than that, they are selling consistency. McDonald's has become the number one fast-food franchise in the world with a 43.8% market share, thanks to the consistency of their service. People go back, again and again, knowing they will always receive the same product and service.

Consumers do not like surprises when making purchases. How many times have you eaten at the same restaurant and had different experiences? One time it was good, the next time it was terrible. That will never happen at McDonald's. They realize how important it is to deliver the same level of service every time. You may or may not like McDonald's food, but you cannot dispute the level of efficiency.

Mercedes is a luxury brand. It is not about the car; it is about what the car says to others. A car is for transportation. A Mercedes is prestige. Anyone can buy a Honda, not everyone can buy a Mercedes.

Home Depot sells selection and price perception. They have convinced consumers that they have everything, and their prices are the best. This does not mean their prices are the best, but consumers believe it to be true. Perception is reality in the mind of the consumer. This makes Home Depot the ultimate one-stop shop for the home.

Buyers have to make an emotional connection to your product or service. People buy on emotion, and the connection they make to your product or service is critical to your success. You must understand the emotional connection you are making to the customer to effectively sell your product or service. What is the emotion that will come up if I ask one of your clients why they buy from you? Are you making an emotional connection powerful enough to motivate the buyer?

People always ask me what I am selling. Many believe I am selling sales training. At no time do I ever think I am selling sales training. I realize how important it is to sell a feeling. The feeling I sell to others is *hope*. I understand the importance of conveying the feeling of hope to the prospect. People will buy from me because they sense that I can help them become more successful and peaceful. This is the feeling of hope I must convey when we are connecting.

Think about the type of emotional connection you want to make with your customer. It may be consistency, trust, reliability, hope, or many others. The important thing is to realize that what you really sell is a feeling, not a thing.

Now pause a moment and describe what you are really selling . . .

ALL SALES MUST BE JUSTIFIED

Every sale requires justification before the purchase can be made. Prospects go through a series of mental cycles before making a final decision. The more expensive the item, the more justification is required to make the buying decision. Think about some of your recent purchases and make a list of how you justified the expense. Ultimately, the purchase must benefit the buyer in some way.

For example, if you purchased a new computer, you may have thought it would make you more productive and efficient, which in turn would help you make more money. That is a great way to justify the purchase.

Look at the following list of the top ten purchase justifiers. Think about what you are selling and determine how many of these justifiers you are touching on when you present your product or service. If you are not hitting on at least three, your sales presentation is in trouble.

TOP 10 PURCHASE JUSTIFIERS
1. Quality of life. How does your product or service improve the buyer's life? This can be anything from making a job easier to being more comfortable.
2. Pleasure. Is there an aspect of pleasure in what you sell? Look for elements in your product or service that make people feel good.
3. Beautify your home or office. People love to improve their surroundings. Any aesthetics you can focus on will be helpful in this area.

4. Education. Everyone loves to gain knowledge they believe will help them do something better. It is very easy to sell the feeling of improvement to others.

5. Relaxation. We are living in very stressful times, which creates the need for rest and relaxation. How can you help people relieve stress?

6. Entertainment. Technology has been at the edge of the entertainment wave. This is also tied to stress relief (see point 10).

7. Planned purchase. When someone is making a planned purchase, they are more educated and patient. This is generally a larger purchase requiring more thought and research. If you sell this type of product or service, be prepared to deal with a higher-level buyer.

8. Emotional satisfaction. In the end, buyers want to walk away feeling they made a good deal. This has nothing to do with the price they paid. It is all about feeling positive about the purchase they have just made.

9. Replace an existing item. This ties into the planned purchase because it is usually a larger purchase. When someone decides to buy new furniture, they are going to shop around and explore the market. They have more time, in most cases, and are more concerned about making a mistake. These are purchases people live with for some time, and they want to make the right decision.

10. Stress relief. As you can see, the issue of stress has come up multiple times. When you can show this benefit, it is a major positive for the buyer. Be sure to weave in something about how what you are offering will help reduce stress on some level.

Let's take an example. Here's how a financial planner might list her key justifiers:

» Quality of life: Help prospect live a higher lifestyle.
» Education: Prospect feels more informed.
» Planned purchase: Prospect was looking for the right person for some time.
» Emotional satisfaction: Prospect feels he/she did something positive.
» Stress relief: Prospect believes he/she is prepared for the future.

Examine your sales presentation and make sure you are touching on as many of these key justifiers as possible. Justification is like a scorecard for buyers. The more checkmarks they make on the page, the easier their buying decision.

BUYERS LOOK FOR AREAS OF IMPROVEMENT TO MOTIVATE AND JUSTIFY

The desire to improve is a great motivator for people. Everyone is looking for a way to improve their quality of life. Any time you can touch on areas of improvement, you will make the sales process easier. In many cases, you know about these great benefits but you do not convey them to the prospect. Make sure the prospect understands all the ways your product or service can help them improve their lives.

TOP FIVE AREAS OF IMPROVEMENT

1. Intellectual.
2. Physical.
3. Spiritual.
4. Emotional.
5. Social.

These areas of improvement tie into justifiers. They are used by the prospect to make a buying decision. Evaluate your sales presentation and determine how you can help people improve. Once again, we are dealing with the feelings of the buyer. Motivating the buyer on an emotional level should always be your goal.

BUYER TYPES

All sales are emotional, regardless of the type of product or service or the amount of money being spent. In the end, the buying decision is made with varying degrees of emotion. The following is a description of the primary buying types you will encounter. This will help you better understand and relate to the different people you encounter.

EXPRESSIVE—50 PERCENT

These are people who like to express themselves to anyone and everyone who is interested in listening. This is done with clothing, cars, watches, business equipment, stocks, and any other possession that expresses style. They are emotionally invested in every purchase and have to feel good about it.

Expressive types are ego driven and want to make a point. They buy with flair and enjoy making a statement.

This type of person buys a new Mercedes and drives around the neighborhood with the top down to make sure everyone sees him. These are the ego-driven buyers who want the world to know about what they purchased.

IMPULSIVE—20 PERCENT

This group buys on high emotion and less intellect. They see it, they want it, and they buy it without remorse. They are looking for an emotional surge with each purchase and do not care about the ramifications.

One of the best places to see impulse buying is in the supermarket. The checkout line is a dream for the impulse buyer. The primary items on the checkout line are magazines and candy.

Supermarkets know who their customers are and understand the types of items they are most likely to buy. You do not see business or financial magazines in this spot. This is the place for tabloids about celebrities or special diets. These are designed for the women in line. The candy is for the screaming child begging his mother for a candy bar.

We all make impulse purchases on occasion. The true impulse buyer makes this type of purchase most of the time. I always feel a sense of responsibility when dealing with an impulse buyer. My job is to make sure they made the right purchase for their long-term needs.

CONFLICTED—16 PERCENT

These people labor over every decision and never really feel good about the final outcome. They have a hard time justifying any purchase and will need a lot of convincing. This group has to build a strong case before making a purchase.

When dealing with people in conflict, it is important to give them some space, but not too much. They tend to waste a lot of your time. Be firm, concise, and kind at the same time to achieve the best results with this group.

BARGAIN HUNTERS—14 PERCENT

These buyers are price driven and the least emotional of the group. This prospect is always looking for the best deal. Fortunately, they are the smallest group in the buyer universe. These are usually well-informed people with a strong desire to be right.

These are also ego-driven buyers who take great pride in being smarter than everyone else. Attempting to battle with these people is a grave mistake. Let them be right, and make the deal that is best for you.

It is important to understand buyer types when developing your sales process. In many industries, a particular type of buyer will appear more often. Understanding the different types will help you make the proper adjustments and help your prospects feel more comfortable.

JUSTIFYING YOUR POSITION

The nature of the buyer creates situations that have a tendency to place salespeople on the defensive. Prospects are conditioned to question you in an effort to discover a weakness they believe will give them an advantage. Your ability to answer these questions without justifying your position is critical to your success. Any time you allow a prospect to put you on the defensive, you are at a distinct disadvantage.

Many prospects have been encouraged, by weak salespeople, to use this tactic to secure a better deal. Susan owns a commercial production company. Her company produces television commercials for small to mid-size businesses. The base rates are $20,000 and up, depending on the difficulty of the production. Every person she sees is looking for the best deal. As a result, they shop the competition and receive quotes ranging from $2,500 to $50,000 and up.

A typical prospect will ask Susan, "Why are you so much more expensive than the other guy I saw?" At this point, Susan goes on the defensive and begins the justification process. She justifies her price by bashing the competition and praising herself.

There are two important rules to remember in this situation:

1. Never bash the competition (it's very unprofessional).
2. Never justify your quality and price.

You can avoid justification by handling situations before they arise. The first step is establishing credibility by showing the quality of your work and having strong testimonials. The next step, much more important, is the feeling or vibe you send to the prospect. If you are constantly getting price resistance, you are not conveying a feeling of confidence to the prospect.

People can feel your level of confidence. If you are not 100 percent confident in your product, service, and price, that uncertainty comes across to the prospect. You attract certain types of prospects based on how you feel about yourself. The better you feel, the less resistance you will receive. Answer questions but avoid becoming defensive. Believe in what you sell, and all of these problems will disappear.

15

DESIGNING A WINNING SALES PROCESS

There are three components to becoming a great salesperson: knowing yourself, knowing your customer, and working with a process. Successful people understand their own strengths and weaknesses. They realize that to be successful they must leverage their strengths and get help in areas where they are weak.

The importance of understanding your customer was outlined in Chapter 13. When you understand the buyer, you become intuitive and dramatically increase your effectiveness. Creating a process allows you to duplicate success with less effort. When you know what works, all you have to do is follow those predetermined steps. Instead of reinventing the wheel each time, you simply flow with proven methods that guarantee results.

Legendary psychologist Carl Jung was one of the first to work in the area of personality types. Jung developed a personality typology that has become so popular that some people don't realize he did anything else! It begins with the distinction between *introversion* and *extroversion*. Introverts are people who prefer an internal world of thoughts, feelings, fantasies, dreams, and so on, while extroverts prefer the external world of things and people, and activities.

The four personality types described in this section are based on Jung's work. It is important to understand that even though people are all unique, they are also all the same on some level. This is not an exact science, but it does give you a framework for personality types.

You will encounter many different personalities in the sales environment. It is important that you identify and adjust to these styles. One key to making sales is to make people feel comfortable. The prospect is much more receptive if he is relaxed.

These are the four basic personality styles:

1. Thinker: logical, structured, planned, organized, conservative.
2. Feeler: likes human interaction; spontaneous, warm, social.
3. Intuitor: imaginative, creative, unstructured, idea-oriented; hates bureaucracy.
4. Sensor: competitive, assertive, demanding, action-oriented, practical.

Although you may see a little of each of these types in yourself, determine which is most and least like your style.

Most like you: _____ Least like you: _____

Because you are predominantly like one of these personalities, you have a 25 percent chance of being the same type as the person to whom you are selling. That means you have a 75 percent chance of *not* being like that person.

Let's assume, for the purpose of this example, that you are a Feeler. You like people and enjoy becoming friends with your clients. When you are selling to another Feeler, it's a wonderful world.

What happens when the Feeler is selling to the Thinker? This is trouble because the Feeler wants to be friends and the Thinker has absolutely no interest in talking about anything other than the facts and the business at hand.

What can you do? I do not advocate being a phony, so I am not going to suggest that you act like a Thinker. I am going to suggest that you temper your personality and make adjustments to the person with whom you are dealing. If you try to become a Thinker, it will be obvious that you are faking it. Be yourself. Simply make a slight personality adjustment to make the prospect feel more comfortable.

If you are at the prospect's office, you can get a sense of what type they are by looking around.

» *The Thinker* will have a very organized, neat, and conservative space. Bare walls and a bit of a cold feeling are common. The Thinker thrives on knowing everything and remaining one step ahead of everyone else.

» The Feeler's space will be the opposite and will include family photos, novelty items, and a much warmer environment. You may see pillows, a lamp, and other items you would expect to find in a living room.

» *The Intuitor* is the more creative and the space will reflect that feeling. The space will be disorganized, colorful, and filled with creativity. Intuitors are not concerned about being able to find a document. They are far more involved with color and all things creative.

» *The Sensor* is very competitive, and that will be on display. Trophies, plaques, awards, and photos with the boss at a golf outing are common. These are the people who have to win.

Identify the type you are dealing with and make the necessary adjustments. Remember, your goal is to make the prospect feel comfortable. People buy when they are relaxed.

STEPS TO A SALE

Successful salespeople follow specific steps that can be duplicated. Using a sales process allows you to identify your strengths and weaknesses. It is impossible to identify and eliminate mistakes without a process. Another advantage is the consistency factor. Each time you complete the steps, you will become more confident and successful. Figure 15.1 outlines the basic steps involved in making a sale.

STEP 1: THE FIRST CONTACT

The first time a prospect becomes aware of your business is their first contact with you. This is very important because it sets the tone for the entire relationship. Therefore, it is critical to remain consistent and uniform. Your benefit statement will also play an important role in this step. Do not underestimate the importance of this step. You only get one shot at a first impression, and it will stay with the prospect forever.

There are many ways to make first contact:

- » Direct mail.
- » Print ad.
- » E-mail.
- » Web site.
- » Directory
- » Sign.
- » Business card.
- » Brochure.
- » Telephone.
- » Networking.
- » Referral.
- » Meeting.
- » Speaking.
- » Trade show.
- » Article.

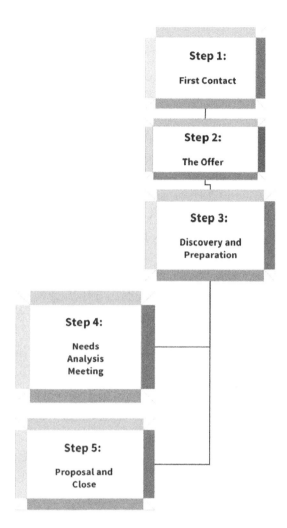

FIGURE 15.1 Steps in Making a Sale

As you can see, this list could go on forever. There are many ways a potential client encounters your business. This initial contact or *touch*, as it is called in the sales world, is critical. It immediately creates an image in the mind of the prospect. Rude secretaries have ruined more sales deals than I can calculate.

People receive this initial contact through one (or more) of three avenues: visual, auditory, or kinesthetic.

1. *Visual:* A prospect sees something about your company. This could be a business card, ad, web site, or brochure. It could also be you or a salesperson. What they see conveys the image of your company. Having a consistent look and message is very important. All colors, images, and messages must be congruent. Major brands are very consistent, creating instant recognition.

2. *Auditory:* A prospect hears from you or your staff. The first impression is often a voice on the phone. The person answering the phone may be the most important person in your company. People often have a negative association with a company based on a simple telephone transaction. Here are some keys to success in this area:
   » Make sure the phone is always answered with the same greeting.
   » Express the importance of professionalism to anyone who may answer the phone.
   » Capture all relevant information from each caller.
   » Review your process on a regular basis to be sure it is being maintained.

3. *Kinesthetic (feeling):* A feeling is aroused, and the prospect attaches it to your business. It is very important to instill a positive feeling about your company. How do you feel when you think about companies like Federal Express, McDonald's, Microsoft, Amazon, and Starbucks? Just as there is a feeling that is aroused when you think of these companies, so will people also attach a feeling to your company. It is critical that a positive association is created to ensure growth and prosperity.

STEP 2: THE OFFER

Many people get a prospect's attention but fail to move the

relationship to the next level. Do not expect the prospect to initiate the next action. It is your responsibility to move the process forward.

I offer a "FREE 37-Minute Sales Analysis" by phone if you qualify. Making the definitive statements "37-Minute" and "if you qualify" add credibility to my offer. If anyone can get the offer at any time, it isn't special. Many people believe a free offer is enough to get someone interested. In some cases, it is—but why speak to everyone? Making the offer more exclusive by qualifying your prospects will help eliminate people who are not serious. Do not be afraid to create strong, specific offers.

There are many sample offers you can make, including:

» Free consultation/analysis.
» Free trial (always add a time limit).
» Free newsletter.
» E-course
» Free Book.

For example, a client of mine is a Web designer and offers a free analysis of a prospect's home page plus three selected pages. This allows the designer to make suggestions on a limited basis. The amount of time necessary for this evaluation is acceptable to the designer. In the past, my client was evaluating entire sites. This was taking an extremely long time to complete. In most cases, the prospect used the information and never hired the designer. The new system has streamlined the process, improved the closing ratio by 20 percent, and has been less time-consuming.

Before you make an offer, be sure it makes sense from your perspective. If the offer is too good, it may work against your bottom line. The offer is designed to move the relationship to the next level. Test different offers and determine which is the most effective. I am always trying new offers and testing the market. You never know when you will hit on a phenomenal new offer. The only way to find out is through trial and error.

STEP 3: DISCOVERY AND PREPARATION

Before you go on an appointment, it is important to qualify the prospect. Time is your most valuable asset, and wasting time chasing the wrong people will cost you dearly. If the prospect is in the low-interest category, do not waste your time. Focus on people who are interested in what you offer.

To make sure the prospect is truly interested, prepare a few qualifying questions to ask over the phone. Design these qualifying questions to suit your industry. Here are some sample questions that you can customize to fit your situation.

> » Which product or service are you interested in?
> » When do you plan to make this purchase?
> » What is your budget for this project?
> » Are you currently using the product or service?

The next step is categorizing the prospect. This will help you do a better job of preparing for the appointment. Each prospect will fall into one of three categories. Knowing the proper category before you meet the prospect will give you a major advantage. This information will also determine how you approach the prospect.

1. *New.* This is a prospect who has never purchased your type of product or service. He or she will need more information to move forward.
2. *Current.* This prospect is currently purchasing the product or service you sell from another company.
3. *Tried it before.* This prospect has tried your product or service before but was dissatisfied with the results.

Pay attention as the prospect gives you this information. As you are asking qualifying questions, prospects will inevitably mention their category if you give them sufficient opportunity to speak. For example, they may tell you, "We are using another vendor but will be interested in what you have to say," which puts them in the category of "current."

This information is extremely valuable to you as a salesperson. It gives you a deeper insight into the mentality of the prospect. You will also have a preview of the challenges you will face when you arrive.

Which of the three categories do you think will be the easiest to sell? Most people believe "new" prospects are easiest to sell because they have never used the product or service and there is no competition to knock out. In reality, the new one is the most difficult to sell for the very reason that they have never used or spent money on the product or service before. This type of prospect will require a lot of education and value-building.

Let's look at all three categories and diagnose the different situations.

A *new* prospect has never used the item, so they must be confident to spend money on something they have not purchased before.

Selling this prospect requires a long list of benefits to support the buying decision. You must create a need that they either do not see or have been unable to justify. Identify the main issue and resolve that problem.

When I was selling advertising space, I encountered many people who had never spent a dime on marketing. These old-school business owners saw advertising as a waste of money. One of our competitors designed a program for these non-marketers. He offered them four weeks in his paper—free, with no obligation. If they were happy, they could renew and become paying customers. If not, they could walk away and pay nothing.

This was a no-lose situation for these business owners. Most of them jumped on this opportunity to receive free ads. A salesman who worked for the paper that had made the offer told me that an amazing 70 percent of these people converted to paying customers.

When you are willing to put your money where your mouth is, amazing things can happen. There is always a risk with deals like this, but they can be extremely effective.

A *current* customer must be ready to leave his or her vendor and switch to you. If the customer is unhappy, this could be a very easy sale. If the customer likes the current vendor, you will have to be very compelling.

One strategy is to offer a free sample or allow the prospect to try your service before making a commitment. This is a show of good faith and an excellent way to get your foot in the door. If you are confident about your product or service, a free trial should not be an issue. Once the prospect experiences what you have to offer, they will be willing to make the switch. Search for what their current vendor is *not* doing and fill that gap. Look for pain and be the doctor on call. If you can relieve pain or a problem better than your competition, you will get the business.

The *tried it before* customer is the easiest to sell. They have already demonstrated interest in what you have to sell and have shown that they are willing to pay for it. You have to figure out what went wrong with the previous experience and address those concerns. Once again, we are looking for pain or the previous issues that caused the problem. Solve their problems and the business is yours.

BE PREPARED

There is nothing worse than a salesperson who is unprepared. Most sales are made or lost in the preparation process. If you do your homework before the meeting, your chances of closing the deal will increase dramatically.

Good preparation should become part of your sales process. This is one of the best habits a salesperson can develop. As your business grows, it's easy to forget to prepare. You may think preparation is no longer a necessary part of your sales process. Do not become complacent. Good preparation never goes out of style.

An important aspect of preparation is product and industry knowledge. The more you know, the easier it is to remain in a current state of readiness. Make sure you are up to date on industry information and market trends. Knowledge is your greatest weapon in the information age. Do not get caught off guard by missing key details in the market.

One of my favorite quotes comes from Joe Paterno, the legendary football coach at Penn State University. Joe said, "The will to win is important but the willingness to prepare is vital."

PREPARATION TIPS

» Go to the company's website and find out as much about the business as possible.
» On a search engine, conduct a keyword search for both the company and the person you are going to see. You will find press releases and other valuable information about the company.
» Find out as much as possible about the person you are going to see. You can speak to other people in the industry or other vendors.
» Make sure you have a clear understanding of the prospect's project.
» Prepare the materials necessary for the specific area of business you are attempting to sell. Do not go overboard and barrage the prospect with too much information.

STEP 4: THE NEEDS ANALYSIS MEETING

One of the great failings of many salespeople is not addressing what the prospect really needs. Many salespeople feel compelled to tell the prospect about what they do. The problem is that prospects only care about how they are going to benefit. Focus on what you can do for them—*why they need you*.

In the needs analysis meeting, you should employ the 70/30

rule: The prospect should be speaking 70 percent of the time, and the salesperson should be speaking only 30 percent of the time.

Your goal is to find out where the prospect is experiencing pain. Almost 90 percent of all purchases are made to relieve pain. Focus your attention on the problems the prospect is attempting to solve.

Prepare your questions in advance. Part of your sales process is creating a sales questionnaire. This questionnaire will be used again and again as you refine your sales process. All questions should be designed to bring out the key areas of distress.

Many salespeople feel compelled to tell the prospect about all the different things they can do to help. In most cases, the prospect is only interested in one or two of the products or services you offer. All salespeople should see themselves as doctors. Your job is very simple: Identify and relieve my pain.

How would you feel if you walked into a doctor's office and he or she said, "Don't tell me what your problem is—let me guess"? I don't think you would be too happy with this approach to your health. Yet this is the approach many salespeople take when speaking to potential clients.

The first thing a doctor says to you is, "Where does it hurt?" She then checks that specific area to determine the best course of action. This is exactly what should happen in a selling situation. Zero in on a specific problem and tell the prospect how you can help solve it.

When you are asking questions, it is important to be sincere. Your energy reflects how you feel when asking these questions. If you are truly interested, the prospect feels your concern and reacts by being attracted to you. When you are just going through the motions, you are vibrating a completely different feeling. Prepare questions that will help you find the issues the prospect is facing.

As you continue to refine the process and questions, you will begin to know the answers before the prospect says them. This is a true sign that you are becoming more intuitive in your sales process. It is important that you allow prospects to tell you about their issues. You may know the answers, but they have to express the need first. This is where your ability to *shut up* will become extremely valuable. I do not mean to be harsh by saying "shut up," but you must learn to let those on the other side of the desk express themselves.

The information you collect will be used to create your proposal. The proposal will focus on resolving all key problems and making life easier for your client. Make your next appointment before you leave. Be sure to give yourself enough time to prepare for the next meeting. If you need three days to complete the proposal, add at least two buffer days. This gives you extra time in the event of an unforeseen issue.

STEP 5: THE PROPOSAL AND CLOSE

At this point, the actual deal should be just a formality. I always feel that closing is the easiest part of the selling process. Creating quality selling opportunities is far more difficult. Your proposal should address all of the issues the client has previously expressed. In many cases, the pricing options have already been discussed.

Present your solutions and benefits one by one. Be sure the prospect understands the value you are offering. Too many times I see salespeople breeze over key benefits as if they had no value. All great salespeople are frustrated actors. Use that skill to romance and build value into your proposal. Do not rush or feel pressured at this point.

You should feel very relaxed, knowing you have the perfect solution.

Once you have presented the benefits and answered all questions, it is time to close the deal. I always ask, "Do you have any other questions?" before handing the contract to the prospect to be signed. This helps to avoid an awkward situation before the deal is finished. At this point, you must let the moment breathe and allow the prospect to look over the agreement. The most important thing right now is silence. Do not speak again unless the prospect has a question. The next thing you should hear is, "Thank you. When do we begin?"

Track your closing ratio to check your progress. As you improve your sales system, you will see the sales numbers and closing ratios improve. Always evaluate each presentation and look for strengths and weaknesses. Your sales process will be in a constant state of flux as you continue to improve.

LET'S TALK ABOUT RETAIL

The sales process in the retail environment may be less formal, but solid systems will still have a dramatic effect on sales. Many retailers believe that people come in, look around, and buy what they want. They place a tremendous amount of importance on displays, product placement, and window dressing. All these elements are important in the retail environment.

But there will also be some level of personal interaction in any retail situation. A well-run retailer always wins the sales game. Having professional people who are trained properly will make a dramatic difference. Imagine if every customer spent an extra 10 percent because the person on the floor was able to assist them in a professional manner.

Retailers sometimes complain that training salespeople is a major investment in time and resources, but they are blind to the potential benefits. If you process 100 transactions per day at $25 each, you would have $2,500 in sales. Add 10 percent, or $250 per day, then multiply by 365 days. You now have an additional $91,250 in annual revenue. All you need is better sales training and attention to detail.

Years ago my wife decided to leave her sales job and become a makeup artist. She worked at the cosmetics counter of a major department store. She was well-trained in product knowledge but received virtually no sales training.

Each month she would outsell the other women at the counter by 30 percent or more. The reason for this dramatic difference was my wife's sales background. The other women were handing people what they ordered. My wife would always ask if they wanted an additional item. "Would you like the lipstick that goes with that nail polish?" was a standard line for her.

Every person in your organization is a salesperson. If they encounter clients, they have an effect on sales. In the retail world, there are countless opportunities to improve your average sale and increase volume. Train your people and make them understand their importance to the business.

16

BUILDING YOUR LEAD FUNNEL SYSTEM

Having the best service and sales process in the world is critical to your long-term success. Unfortunately, service and process do not mean very much if you do not have any prospects to sell. This chapter focuses on how to create multiple lead sources. You will learn to create the lead funnels necessary to maintain a steady cash flow. These funnels are at the core of the Attractor Sales System™.

Each funnel you use must become part of your sales system. That is why I suggest adding one at a time and incorporating it into your sales culture. These funnels only work if you are consistent. You can't try one for a month and then jump to another. They take time to implement and perfect before showing results.

Most people do not give each funnel enough time to mature. This results in wasted time and energy. If you are not willing to commit to a particular funnel, do not start in that area.

This chapter describes the various funnels and how to use them properly. It is not necessary to use them all to be successful. Select the funnels that work best for your business and get started today. Little by little these funnels will begin to produce high-quality leads for your business. Once the system is working, all you have to do is manage it. Eventually, you will never have to worry about new business again.

THE DATABASE FACTOR

The most important aspect of the Attractor Sales System™ is your database. Building your database is critical to long-term success. It is an ongoing project that will be a cornerstone of your growth. Most business comes from someone who already knows your company. Your database should consist of active clients, inactive clients, and all other contacts.

Building the Attractor Sales System™ requires a solid group of loyal clients who buy from you again and again. People buy from people they know and trust. It takes a lot of work to build a high level of trust with clients. Once you have accomplished this, it is critical to leverage that relationship.

Virtually every successful career has established a loyal fan population; every great business has a loyal customer base. In Hollywood, top actors, from a financial perspective, are called bankable stars. Years ago, I saw a top Hollywood agent defining this concept. He said, "Robert De Niro is a great actor, but Eddie Murphy is a movie star." What he meant was that while a new De Niro movie may be great, that does not mean it will do well at the box office. Conversely, a new Eddie Murphy film is guaranteed to do well financially because Eddie's fans will turn out and pay money to see anything he does. Eddie Murphy has fans. Robert De Niro has admirers. It is nice to have admirers, but they don't pay the rent. You need fans who are willing to pay you for your product or service. Not every person in your database will begin as a fan. Most will start as admirers and must be cultivated over time before they reach fan status. The key to moving people from admirers to fans is visibility. Part of the lead funnel process revolves around remaining visible. The more admirers you have, the better. Each admirer is a client in waiting.

Having a better business or product than your competition will not guarantee your success. If your competitor has a more loyal fan base, they will always outperform you. It has nothing to do with who is better. "Better" is a matter of judgment. What really determines success is who the client goes to when they want to make a purchase.

You must create a system to monitor and update your database. Use a specific timetable to assure you are consistent. You may decide to add new names once a week or once a month. In either case, select a time frame that works and remain true to that schedule.

THE 14 LEAD FUNNELS
Starbucks Meetings

Once or twice a week, meet with someone on your contact list for coffee. I am sure there are dozens, even hundreds, of people in your contact list whom you have not seen in some time. Go through your Outlook or whatever you use to maintain your contacts. Look for contacts who are not necessarily current or former clients. They may be associates, friends, former coworkers, or others. The intent here is to remain visible and on people's radar screens.

If you are not visible, people will forget about you. In addition, many people may not be aware of some of the new things you are doing. These meetings will result in more leads and opportunities. You will have the opportunity to help these associates as well. It becomes a win-win situation for all.

This is a successful strategy because people are not committing to lunch. Asking someone to lunch is more difficult because it takes time to coordinate. Most people are more willing to meet for a quick cup of coffee. This is the easiest—and in many ways the best, dollar-for-dollar—funnel in my arsenal. Be consistent and be sure to schedule at least one meeting per week.

A woman attending one of my seminars could not wait to use this strategy. She called me a week later and explained how she had closed two deals within a week, using this strategy. It is easy, fun, and a great way to keep in touch with friends.

Newsletter

Sending out a newsletter on a regular basis is a great way to keep your name in front of clients and prospects. You can accomplish this through e-mail or in a conventional print format. E-mail is much less expensive and will allow you to send information more frequently. There are a number of great programs on the market that offer templates and database management applications. One of the most popular is Constant Contact.

Another benefit of newsletters is that you are sending information instead of selling something. Clients and prospects enjoy getting information with no strings attached. It creates goodwill and builds credibility. Your database is a key component in this area. That is why it is so critical to continue working on it all the time.

Many people express reservations about writing a newsletter. They tell me, "I am not a writer and I have no idea how to go about writing something like that." Your newsletter does not have to be *War and Peace*. Think of the *USA Today* format for your newsletter. Send pertinent information in short, digestible bites.

Some of my clients have turned their newsletters into a company project. Each month people submit articles for the newsletter. Getting their articles included has become an honor.

I have a client in the document imaging business who started sending out a newsletter. He had a database of over 4,000 names and was in contact with less than 100 on a regular basis. He was reluctant to use this strategy, but I convinced him it was a good idea. We continued to send the newsletter month after month without seeing any sales. People would send in comments, but no sales could be traced back to the newsletter. The owner was ready to stop when he received an order for over $250,000 for a piece of equipment from someone he had never sold to before. The client said the newsletter was the reason he learned about the company and made the purchase. Now the owner loves his monthly newsletter.

Regular frequency is important with newsletters. Publish as often as once a week, but no less than once a month. Once you commit to a schedule, stick to it. Again, we go back to the consistency issue with all funnels.

Buzz Referrals

Most organizations attempt to create referral programs based on incentives. Although some of these can be effective, most are inconsistent at best. I remember my former insurance agent calling me to ask for a list of people I thought would be interested in speaking with him. This made me very uncomfortable. He is no longer my insurance agent.

Buzz referrals are generated when people feel excited about your work. These referrals are created when you make an impact on people's lives. To stimulate these referrals, you must make yourself valuable without the intention to sell. This is accomplished by providing value with purpose.

Try the following buzz referral stimulators:

» Send relevant articles.
» Email people with a hot tip or idea.
» Refer to a great resource.
» Send business to them.
» Send a card for no reason.
» Tell them about a special event.
» Send a book.
» Invite them to an educational seminar.

When you engage in these activities on a regular basis, people can't wait to refer you. With buzz referrals, you are never asking for a referral. They simply come to you because you are a valuable resource that others want to share.

Speaking

Speaking in front of an audience of potential clients is very powerful. You will create rapport, demonstrate credibility, and establish your brand, all at the same time. Look for associations and other groups that meet on a regular basis. These groups must have members who are potential clients for your business. Organizations such as Chambers of Commerce and Rotary Clubs are always looking for speakers. Expos and trade shows are other great places to speak. There may also be groups in your industry that allow speakers.

One of the greatest benefits of speaking in front of a group is compressing time. Your message can reach dozens or even hundreds of people in less than an hour. As a comparison, how long would it take for you to see thirty people on a one-on-one basis?

When I started this business, I built virtually my entire database through speaking. I did not have a lot of money for marketing and found speaking to be a great way to spread my message and create buzz. This is one of the fastest ways to accelerate your business and generate more qualified leads.

If you are not comfortable speaking in front of a group, what are you doing in sales in the first place? There are many organizations that can help you, including Dale Carnegie and Toastmasters International.

Public or Industry-Specific Seminars

With this funnel, you host your own public seminar. This requires a great deal of effort, including much work marketing the event. I would suggest tackling a public seminar only after you have done a number of speaking engagements. The public seminar is a great marketing tool for the right industry. I built my entire business using this particular funnel.

One of my clients, a mortgage broker, has done several successful seminars in this active real estate market. His seminars target people who are buying or refinancing a home. The key is creating a topic that will get attention. Remember you are trying to motivate people to disrupt their schedules and come to an event. You need a strong topic to drive people in the door.

Certain benefit themes work very well, such as helping them learn how to:

» Increase efficiency.
» Save money.
» Save time.
» Make extra money.
» Cut costs.

Motivate people with benefits and tell them why your event is so special. You must prepare an offer at the end of the presentation to move people into your sales process.

Teleseminars and Webinars

The teleseminar/webinar model will expand your market and visibility. Teleseminars and webinars involve the same concepts as public seminars, but they are conducted over the phone or by computer. A teleseminar is a big conference call and can be conducted from any location.

To conduct a teleseminar or webinar, you will need a platform to conduct your session. With seminars and webinars, it is important to create a smooth registration process. People should be able to register online to assure the best results. You can also offer a teleseminar or webinar to existing clients as an added value.

Apply the same rules and seek the same benefit-driven topics as public seminars. The main difference here is that you are not limited by geography. People can call in from anywhere, which expands your market geographically.

Key Groups and Organizations

Within your target or vertical markets there are many groups and organizations. Since it is more productive to send your message to many people at the same time, becoming visible to these organizations is a good way to find new business.

One of my clients installs carpeting in commercial buildings. He is involved in all the building management organizations in his target market. Building managers make the buying decisions, and there are hundreds in this group. Seek out the key groups in your market and make yourself visible.

There are two types of key groups: groups specific to your field, and groups who purchase the product or service you sell. Be sure you are visible in both, especially the groups that have members that can buy from you.

Client Education

People love to learn how to be more productive. Teach your clients how to use your product or service and tell them about all the other aspects of your business. This can be done with a small group in a conference room, teleseminar, or webinar. Offer breakfast or lunch to create a positive atmosphere and promote goodwill.

This is also an opportunity to tell clients about new products and services. Use your newsletter to educate and inform clients. You can also send out a mailing or direct them to a new page on your website.

Do not underestimate the importance of keeping your clients and prospects informed. Sending pertinent information and remaining visible is very powerful for your business.

Writing Articles

Having articles published in trade magazines, newspapers, and online will create visibility and build your credibility. Submit articles to as many publishers as possible in your industry. Your website will often also be linked to the publisher's website which will bring more Internet traffic to you.

Look for publications relevant to your industry and clients. There are many *ezines* (online magazines) that are constantly looking for articles. Go to your favorite search engine and type in "ezines." You will see many directories and information regarding these publications.

Trade Shows

The right trade show can be a gold mine of opportunity. However, most salespeople fail to follow up after the show. People leave with hundreds of contacts, and then never speak to these people again.

Make sure you have a strong offer in place and a system to capture names. You must also have a plan of attack to maximize the leads you collect at a show. Many companies spend a fortune going to shows and then neglect to follow through. A trade show is also a great source of contacts for your database.

Joint Ventures

Joint ventures are one of the most powerful, yet often overlooked, strategies in the market. A joint venture is a mutual agreement to promote products or services. Major corporations have been involved in joint ventures for years as they leverage each other's brands. I recently received a promotion from Circuit City and Pizza Hut. Postcards were available at both stores offering a chance to win a flat-screen TV and a year's supply of pizza. To qualify, you had to go to a specific site and enter your contact information.

Pizza Hut was also promoting a Pizza Hut Card, a gift card for pizza. The purpose of this promotion was to generate traffic at stores and to build the company's databases. Both companies now have the prospect's information that they can use to market other offers.

The key to success with joint ventures is finding good partners. I deal with a number of different markets including small to mid-size businesses and look for people who are working with my market but do not compete. My list of partners includes accountants, networking organizations, lawyers, marketing firms, Web designers, Chambers of Commerce, other trainers, consultants, and product sellers.

This is where your database has real value. You can offer to send a message to your database regarding the partner's business in exchange for leads or a reciprocal promotion. When executed correctly joint, ventures can become your most valuable lead source.

You can also execute joint ventures online. These are called affiliate programs. This type of program is very effective when you are selling a product. It also works well when promoting events and seminars.

When looking for partners, it is important to select people who share your beliefs and standards. This is not about finding the person with the best list or the most money. You have to find partners you are excited about. This is not a quantity game but a quality game. Do not rely on e-mail alone to create these partnerships. Pick up the phone and get to know the people behind the sites and businesses you see. This is the best way to determine if they are the right person for you.

Every joint venture I have been involved with has been based on liking the person I spoke to on the phone. Reach out and make contact with partners. You should be adding new partners on a regular basis.

The Internet
Most businesses have websites, but how many have sites that

drive business? Unfortunately, most sites do not even build the database. There are two keys to exploiting the Web as a service seller: Make a great offer and capture names.

I offer a free sales analysis and e-book, which generates leads every day. The key to a good offer is giving prospects what they need. If they are ready, they will take you up on your offer.

If they are not ready, you need a different offer that will capture their information. Offer a free e-course or e-book, or other valuable information. Turn your site into a profit center by making offers to prospects. At the very least, you want to capture a name for your database.

The free offers should be visible on your home page and easy to use. I offer a free e-course, newsletter, or premium item on all of my sites. Be creative with your offers and give people real value. There are a lot of choices online, so you must make a compelling offer with real benefits to capture a new admirer.

Sequential Direct Mail

Direct mail is alive and well, regardless of what people say. Have you checked your mailbox lately? See my point?

There is a direct mail technique that is extremely effective for small businesses and service sellers. It is called *sequential mailing* and it revolves around selecting a specific mailing list and being consistent.

This system is based on the rule of seven, which states, "I have to see your name seven times before I respond." Businesses often send out one mailing and make a determination regarding its success or failure. But you cannot make this determination with only one mailing. Sequential mailing is designed to send a different message to the same people multiple times. This technique results in higher response rates for each mailing. Some of my clients sent the same message over and over again and have achieved an outstanding response.

My personal favorite is sending postcards offering a free sales analysis and directing them to the website. You can also have them call you to receive the special offer.

The mailing list and the copy are critical to your success. Be sure you have a solid database that is targeted to your client profile. In most cases, you have to test a few different ideas to determine which generates the best response.

Public Relations

Getting publicity is a powerful way to gain credibility and exposure. This can be accomplished on a local, regional, national, or international level, depending on your market. You can begin by simply posting information on websites and in publications. Some postings are picked up by news organizations and other media.

The best way to research this information is through search engines. Find all the trade publications and sites that report on your industry. Ask them if you can post information about seminars, new products, or any other points of interest. These postings are free and, in many cases, will generate links back to your site.

You can also contact the publisher or editor and ask for an interview. You will need a good story, like, "I just wrote a new book about ." You may have a new product or service that is relevant to the industry. Remember, these people need content every day to produce their products.

The best place to start is your local town paper. Look for a good hook (story) to tell about your business. You may be running a fund-raiser or have another special offering. Local papers are always looking for a good story.

You can also send press releases regionally, nationally, or internationally at **www.prnewswire.com**.

Figure 16.1 is a diagram of all fourteen funnels discussed here.

FIGURE 16.1 The Funnel System

PLANNING AND EXECUTION

You cannot execute all fourteen of these funnels at one time. Look at the list and select one or two to get started. Each one takes time to develop and adjust to achieve optimum results. The database becomes the key element to the entire plan before you begin.

This system will only work if you are committed and consistent. When you decide to send a monthly newsletter, you have to do it every month. It will not work if you jump in and out of each funnel. Before you commit to a funnel be sure you are willing to see it through to completion.

The easiest way to build this system is to use a calendar. Write down which funnel(s) you want to add in each month.

The calendar will help you plan and remain focused on the objective.

Keep track of your results and make the proper adjustments. This plan is guaranteed to work if you remain consistent and committed. In no time at all, you will see more leads than ever before. This system takes time to develop but it pays dividends for years to come. It is a simple matter of planning and execution.

17

ADDING A LITTLE
MARKETING POLISH

Sales and marketing have always been joined at the hip. The best salespeople are those who know how to market themselves in the most efficient manner. Old-school salespeople did not see the importance of marketing for long-term success. It always amazes me when there is discord between the marketing and sales departments of an organization.

As a salesperson or entrepreneur, you are always positioning yourself and marketing to potential clients. I have seen salespeople pay assistants, out of their own pockets, to work in marketing and lead generation. It is imperative to always remain in a marketing mindset.

Writing has become very important in today's world of business, largely due to the Internet. You are always sending e-mails, notes, and proposals. Much of your writing will have an element of ad copy pizzazz. You may also be sending out mail or writing print ads. Learning to effectively write copy for all media will be a tremendous benefit to your business.

All successful marketing begins and ends with copy. You need great ad copy to draw people to your business. A simple change in wording can make the difference between a successful ad and a complete bust. By changing a single word, you can dramatically increase your response rates.

Every word you write carries a vibration of energy, based on both the actual word and how you feel when you are writing it. Some of my most successful marketing campaigns have been very simple and spur of the moment. If you feel good when writing, the words carry that positive energy. Never attempt to write anything when you are not in a flowing state of positive energy. Always connect to your feelings as you write. The better you feel, the better your message will be received.

CREATING A GREAT AD
Your ad has three basic elements:

1. The headline.
2. The body copy.
3. The close.

The Headline
Legendary ad man David Ogilvy always said, "Ninety percent of the success of your ad is based on the headline." The headline is the key because you are competing with everyone else to get attention. The average person sees between 4,000-10,000 advertising messages every day. Think about how many ads you see or hear each day. Television, radio, billboards, buses, Internet, mail, and telemarketing barrage you all day long.

Let's begin with a headline test. The following ads were tested with different headlines. In each pair the ad content was exactly the same except for the headline. Can you select the headline that was most successful? Each of the winning headlines drew more than double the response rate of its alternate. That shows you the power of a strong headline.

As you look at these headlines, quickly select the one that you feel is the most powerful in each pair.

Magazine Ad to Sell Subscriptions
A. How to do your Christmas shopping in 5 minutes
B. The gift that comes 12 times a year

Finance Company Soliciting Loan Applications
A. How to get a $5,000 loan
B. When should your family get a loan?

Selling a Correspondence Course for Interior Design
A. To every woman who would like a career in interior design
B. Can you spot these 7 common decorating mistakes?

Now let's look at the winning headlines and analyze why they received a response more than double that of the others.

In the first ad, the reason that A is more effective is that it conveys a solid *benefit* for any Christmas shopper. Headline B is vague and without a clear benefit. It *sounds* nice, but does it really get you excited? Your goal is to get the reader excited so they will respond. Many copywriters try to be cute instead of results oriented. Let's save cute for our kids and write copy that will get people to buy our product or service.

In the case of the finance company soliciting loan clients, once again we see the difference between being *direct* and trying to be interesting. If I need a loan, headline A is speaking to me. The person responding to this ad is someone who needs a loan. If I am not thinking about a loan, I am not really a good prospect. The bank wants people who are ready to come in and apply for a loan.

In the third ad, although headline A sounds intriguing, it still lacks the bite necessary to get the reader to respond. The winning component in headline B is *involvement*. If you can get the reader involved in your ad, you have a   real winner. You see many ads that say "Circle this" and "Check that" to see if you qualify. These are great techniques that keep the reader's attention on your ad longer and increase response.

Were you able to select the winners? If you answered two of three correctly, you have an eye for advertising. If not, don't worry. Most people usually get one correct at best.

Headline Tips

» Should be as short as possible and concise. (In some cases, a long headline can be effective, but it must be very well written.)
» Must convey a benefit to the reader.
» Must be targeted to your audience (speak to the people in your client profile).
» Has to stand out from other ads.
» Does not try to be cute.
» Avoids long words if possible (they can cause confusion).
» Follows the KISS rule: Keep It Simple, Stupid.

The easiest way to create a great headline is to create a list of the benefits you offer. Use that list as a basis for your headlines.

Here are some of the more popular types of headlines—notice how they are all benefit oriented:

» How to . . .
» Improvement in any area of life.
» Exclusive offer.
» Time dated offer (only available for a short time).
» Time saver.
» Stress relief.
» Gaining pleasure.

The best way to test a headline's effectiveness is with a focus group of friends and family. Write six to twelve headlines and show them to the group. See which headlines get the best response and ask people why they responded to a particular headline.

The Body Copy

The next section in your ad is the body copy. This is the information that follows the headline. When reading ads, most people read the headline and the close; in letters, they read the first paragraph and the postscript.

In the body you tell your story and describe your product or service. Rules similar to creating a headline apply also to the ad body.

The body copy should convey benefit to the reader.

Another good idea is to include testimonials from satisfied customers. Do not underestimate the power of these words. People want to know that others have benefited from your service or product. You may have performed the service while at a salaried or commissioned job. For example, I conducted training programs for employers before going out on my own. I was able to use these companies as sources for testimonials.

One of the biggest mistakes people make is using the ad to tell about themselves. No one cares how great you are or what makes you so wonderful. Instead mention things like, "20 years' experience in the industry," or, "specialist in this field." Avoid "me, me, me" and think about the needs of the prospect.

Another technique I like is using bullets to make specific points. People do not like to read big blocks of copy. Easy-to-read bullet points are much more effective.

The Close

This is where most amateur copywriters make their biggest mistake. They do not close the ad with a call to action. The reader does not know what to do. You have to tell the reader *exactly* what he is supposed to do at the end of your ad.

Assuming the reader knows what to do is a critical mistake.

If you have gotten someone to read your entire ad, they are interested. Failure to close negates all the good work you did to get them to that point.

There are different closes depending upon what you want to accomplish. Your goal may be to get someone to call or to go to your web site. In retail you want people to come to your store with the special offer in hand.

Here are some sample closing lines:

» Call 000-000-0000 today for a FREE consultation.
» Call 000-000-0000 today and receive a FREE gift.
» Go to your site and receive a FREE report.
» (Retail) Use this coupon for $10 OFF your next purchase of $30 or more.

You must give the prospect a reason to make the call, go to the web site, or come to your store. The headline brings them in, and the close tells them what to do.

The two most powerful words in advertising are *free* and *new*. Use these words as much as possible in your copy. Copywriting is one skill that may require outside help. If you do not feel confident that you can write strong copy, hire a writer. This is an important key to your marketing success. Do not be penny-wise and dollar-foolish in this area.

PACKAGING AND UP-SELLS

Maximizing your opportunities requires the ability to use all of the tools available to you. Each sale is a transaction that must be optimized. Every business is transaction-based, and there is a premium on getting the most out of every sale.

Creating Packages

People love to buy packages because they have a perception of higher value. You have also done the thinking for them by grouping products together. The more complicated the purchase is, the longer it will take to complete the deal.

When I was selling cable spots, we had the ability to sell thirty-six channels. Each client had to decide which channels would be the best for their business. This caused a lot of confusion for advertisers. I created package plans based on the demographics of each channel. This allowed the advertiser to select the best package for his or her business. Figure 17.1 lists some of the sample packages I put together.

Sports	Children	Upscale
ESPN	Nickelodeon	A&E
ESPN 2	Cartoon Network	History Channel
FOX Sports	Disney	Food Network
Classic Sports	ABC Family	Discovery

FIGURE 17.1 Sample Cable Packages

Bundle Services/Products
Another good technique is bundling items together. You can use this strategy with services or products or a combination of the two. The higher the perceived value, the easier it is to sell your product or service.

McDonald's does a great job of packaging with its various meals. You can order a sandwich, fries, and a drink by using a number.

There are unlimited combinations with regard to packaging. Here are a few examples:

Web Design (service)
» Home page design
» Five buttons

» Ten pages of content
» One year of support

Computer System (product)
» Tower
» Monitor
» Printer
» Cables
» Software

Sales Training (product and service)
» Home study course
» Six training sessions
» One year of e-mail support

You can also create multiple packages at different price points. This will help you expand your market. You may have a basic package for $250 and an advanced plan for $2,000.

Creating a new package also gives you a reason to call clients. This is a great way to build relationships and reactivate former clients. Start planning your new packages today. This will help you increase your average sale and build volume.

Up-Sells

Up-selling means adding something to a sale you have already completed. This is a very common technique in direct response advertising and infomercials. If you order a product through an infomercial, the operator will try to sell you additional items.

I purchased a piece of exercise equipment, and the operator took me through a series of offers. All the offers were related to making the product better or more useful. The beauty of an up-sell is that it is all profit. You have already made the sale and incurred the cost of the transaction.

An article in *ADWEEK* reported, 25 percent of all infomercial buyers will purchase the up-sell. This can be extremely profitable for your business. Imagine if 25 percent of your clients purchased an additional product or service every time you made a sale. That profit goes directly to your bottom line. This is an easy way to add revenue in a hurry.

Keys to a good up-sell:

» It makes sense and complements the main purchase.
» It makes the main product/service more valuable.
» It has a highly perceived value.
» It can be used immediately.

Let's look at another example of an up-sell. A local music store created a package that included a guitar, an amplifier, a case, and headphones, all for $269. The up-sell they offered was "50 percent off your first three lessons—only $30 (regular price $60)."

This is a great up-sell because if the student is happy, she will then continue the lessons at the regular price. The store owner told me the average student spends $500 per year. Look at the numbers, outlined in Figure 17.2. As you can see, the up-sell offer generated $900 in initial sales plus another $7,500 in long-term sales. This does not include additional purchases by students and the referrals the teachers are sure to receive.

Packages Sold	Price	Total Revenue
100	$269	$26,900
Up-Sells @ 30%	Price	Total Revenue
30	$30	$900
Long-Term Students	Price	Total Revenue
15	$500	$7,500

FIGURE 17.2 Effects of Guitar Up-Sell for Music Store

Start to work on your up-sells today and watch your profits soar. Remember that the up-sells must be prepared and tested. You may have to adjust your offer several times before it takes hold.

There are a few keys to testing your offer. In many cases, people change the offer too often. It may take time before the offer catches on with your market. Another variable is the confidence the salesperson has regarding the offer. If you feel it is not that great of an offer, this will affect how you feel (and the energy you put out) when you deliver it. Make sure you believe the up-sell you are offering is of great value to the client.

There is no such thing as real value. It is all based on the feelings of the salesperson and client. When you believe in your offer, it carries a tremendous level of positive energy to the client. It is very easy to monitor your level of confidence and belief. All you have to do is look at the reaction of the client. If they share your level of enthusiasm, you are conveying a strong belief in your offer.

Guilt is a feeling that comes up in certain up-selling situations. Salespeople have expressed this feeling to me on many occasions. I hear statements such as, "I feel they already bought something, and I do not want to push it." This also connects to a feeling of fear. When a salesperson feels fortunate to have made the sale, a feeling of fear is present.

You must feel that the product or service you sell is helping people. They are buying it because they believe it will improve their lives. If you share that belief, the up-sell is a natural process. When you have doubt, the feelings of fear will surely surface.

Continue to test and adjust until you find an up-sell that works. Remember, the better you feel about it, the more successful you will be. Remain open creatively and continue to add more up-sells and packages. This will have a dramatic impact on your sales and referrals.

18

THE ULTIMATE VICTORY

The world of sales is filled with pressure and high expectations. Your life revolves around numbers and the ability to successfully reach a goal. It can be a world of harsh judgment and criticism. This environment creates tension and high stress levels in many cases. The creed of many organizations is still based on the old "If you can't stand the heat, get out of the kitchen" philosophy.

How do you walk the line between financial prosperity and spiritual power? Is it necessary to focus on winning at all times? Can you remain spiritual, true to yourself, and still become financially successful? Is the ego essential to reach a high level of financial prosperity?

My hope is that you now realize it is possible to remain true to your spirit and experience abundance in all areas of your life. By making the necessary adjustments and clearing negative patterns, you can create the life of your dreams.

When you stop keeping score, your life will become easier and more flowing. This philosophy goes against much of what has been taught in the traditional business sector. Success is usually judged by the numbers. You have to increase market share, improve profit margins, and build volume. Every time you do not meet expectations; you are considered a failure. In many cases, management will use fear of loss as a method of motivation. "If you are unable to make your numbers you will be fired" is the strategy of choice for many companies.

Fear is one of the lowest levels of energy vibration. It is impossible to sustain any level of success while you are fearful. Using this tactic actually has the opposite effect on people. It does not motivate—it paralyzes. Fear also affects the decision-making process. It leads to desperation, which leads to irrational decisions. Making the deal when you do not feel good about it, just to make your number, is fear based. You know when fear is your emotional driver. When you feel fearful, your soul is telling you something. Do not allow fear to dictate how you conduct business.

Another extreme negative in the world of sales is greed. When organizations place money and profit above all else, they are creating an environment of greed. Greed's message is that money is all that matters. When people get caught up in the power of greed, it results in situations like Enron and Tyco. In these cases, the egos involved were obsessed with power and status. These are examples of allowing the ego to use the outside world to create an identity. All negative motivators will ultimately yield a negative outcome.

Can you simply go out and do your own thing without any attachment to numbers? This is the riddle I have set out to solve with this book. The Attractor Sales System™ was designed to help people transcend the ordinary and become extraordinary. When you truly understand and implement this system, all negative concerns will be eliminated. When you are flowing, there is no need to be in a state of worry or fear.

The numbers or financial aspects of the business will always be important and must be monitored, but the key is not to become obsessed with the numbers alone. Pay attention to all aspects of your business or sales career. Your financial success reflects how you truly feel about yourself.

WALKING A PARALLEL PATH

As I became more spiritual, the physical world began to seem less important. The material possessions I had once seen as the ultimate indicators of success paled in comparison to the feelings of peace and joy I felt in an elevated spiritual state. On some level, I had become detached from the physical world and all of its trappings.

I began to drift into feelings of total detachment and wondered what it would be like to be truly removed from society. It seemed to be easier to pursue the power of spiritual enlightenment without all of the distractions of this world. I wondered, was this the path to true enlightenment?

Through meditation I realized that for some this is the right path, but it was not my purpose in this lifetime. My purpose is to teach others how to live in our complex society and still walk in a state of peace. I have discovered that it is possible, although challenging, to live these principles and continue to function in today's world.

The key for me and many others is the understanding that we must always be focusing on the inside. When I see my thoughts drifting to the outside world, I am quick to stop my destructive ideas and look inward. No amount of money or material possessions can compare with the most powerful feelings in the universe. True success can only be measured in love, peace, and joy.

Follow these feelings and you can have everything you desire and more. You can have your cake and eat it, too, if you remain true to yourself. Allow your love to flow and help amplify the energy of this world. When you do, the rewards will be well beyond what you can imagine.

My objective is to walk a *parallel path* each day. We are living in a linear world, and there are certain rules we must follow. Your job is to continue to work on your inner self while continuing to improve your technical skill. This will make you an unstoppable force. Imagine yourself walking this incredible path each day. As your energy vibration becomes clearer, you will feel lighter and more flowing. This clarity will help your conscious mind reach a much higher level of infinite intelligence.

Use the depiction of parallel paths shown in Figure 18.1 to help you stay on track.

See this image in your mind throughout the day. Notice how questions become easier to answer and making the right decision is no longer a challenge. You will become more powerful and filled with light energy. This is a journey like no other. Enjoy every aspect of the trip as each step, no matter how difficult, carries with it a special gift.

One day you will master this process and look back to a time when the smallest step was an incredible challenge. Remain patient—this is an organic process, not a linear one. We are conditioned to believe that everything, especially in business, has a beginning, middle, and end. See yourself as the seed of a flower. Once planted, the seed will grow exactly the way nature intended. There is nothing you can do to make the flower grow faster. The only thing you can do is nurture the seed to assure it will grow to be healthy and strong.

INCREASING SKILL LEVEL/KNOWLEDGE
INCREASING ENERGY VIBRATION

FIGURE 18.1 Walking a Parallel Path

If you attempt to force this process, you will move into a state of resistance. This will block your energy and slow you down. When this happens, you are in an ego state of overthinking. The more you flow, the more smoothly your process will go. Do not try to use logic, as the universe is moving you along in perfect synchronicity.

Every step of your journey has been carefully orchestrated to help you experience the emotions you came here to experience. As you look back at your life, you will realize that all of your growth was the result of working through difficult situations. All of these experiences become useful for the next step in your journey.

Your emotional and spiritual growth have no limitations. You can continue to grow in these areas until the day your work for this specific lifetime is complete. But remember, this is an option, not a given. Many people will choose not to grow much, and that is their right. It is not our job to judge anyone's progress. We are here to do our own work and complete our individual mission. Perhaps we will be fortunate enough to help some others along the way.

Enjoy your newfound power as a Spiritual Seller! Use it wisely and you can have anything you desire in this world. Open your mind to unlimited possibilities.

GLOSSARY OF KEY TERMS

chakras The seven key energy points within your body. These energy points control your vibration of energy.

emotional triggers People, incidents, and situations that bring up key emotional issues.

extension of power The ability to elevate others to a higher level.

flow state Going with the flow and not resisting your feelings.

holding the vibration The ability to maintain a high level of energy vibration at all times.

law of attraction Like energy attracts like energy. You are always vibrating energy, which is constantly attracting and repelling things in your life.

manifesting The ability to focus your thoughts and energy on the things you truly want in life, enabling you to create the situations and opportunities you desire.

space of power Following your true feelings and working from the inside out. You can help others reach a higher level as you extend this power.

Made in United States
Orlando, FL
15 January 2025

57307240R00137